CRAFTS

BOOK CLUB ASSOCIATES

London

in association with Phoebus

Editor: **Mary Harding**
Assistant Editor: **Margo Coughtrie**
Editorial Assistants: **Kitsa Caswell/Sally Fisher**
Consultants: **Greta Barrett/Frances Rogers**
Design Co-ordinator: **Jan Churcher**
Production Control: **Sheila Biddlecombe**
Editorial Director: **Graham Donaldson**

INTRODUCTION

The popularity of handcrafts is greater than ever with more and more people discovering the pleasure of creating something unique in a world of mass-produced objects. This book introduces you to many of the best-loved crafts, all of which require little equipment and can easily be tackled at home.

Take printing and painting for example. A plain fabric can be transformed by the simple, but effective means of linoleum or potato printing or with fabric paints. For découpage, too, all you need are paper cutouts, an old box or tray, and some varnish to change a boring object to one that you will be proud to display.

There are crafts that will beautify your home such as weaving, braiding, or batik. Others, like beadwork and macrame, will provide you with a wardrobe of unusual accessories or a fund of birthday and Christmas presents. There are crafts that are simple enough for children to enjoy, others that will tempt experts to test their skill.

With this book, you will discover that anyone can be creative with the right sort of inspiration. So whether it's beading, painting, weaving, or modelling clay that appeals to you, you'll find plenty to fire your imagination.

This edition published 1978 by
Book Club Associates
By arrangement with Phoebus Publishing Company
Reprinted in 1980

Produced in Hong Kong by
Mandarin Offset Ltd

CONTENTS

Clay modelling	6
Iron-on appliqué	9
Plastic crafts	12
Paper crafts	18
Nature crafts	31
Beading	34
Printing	48
Painting	54
Batik	74
Dyeing yarn	80
Weaving	83
Braiding	98
Macrame	108
Leatherwork	120
Index	127

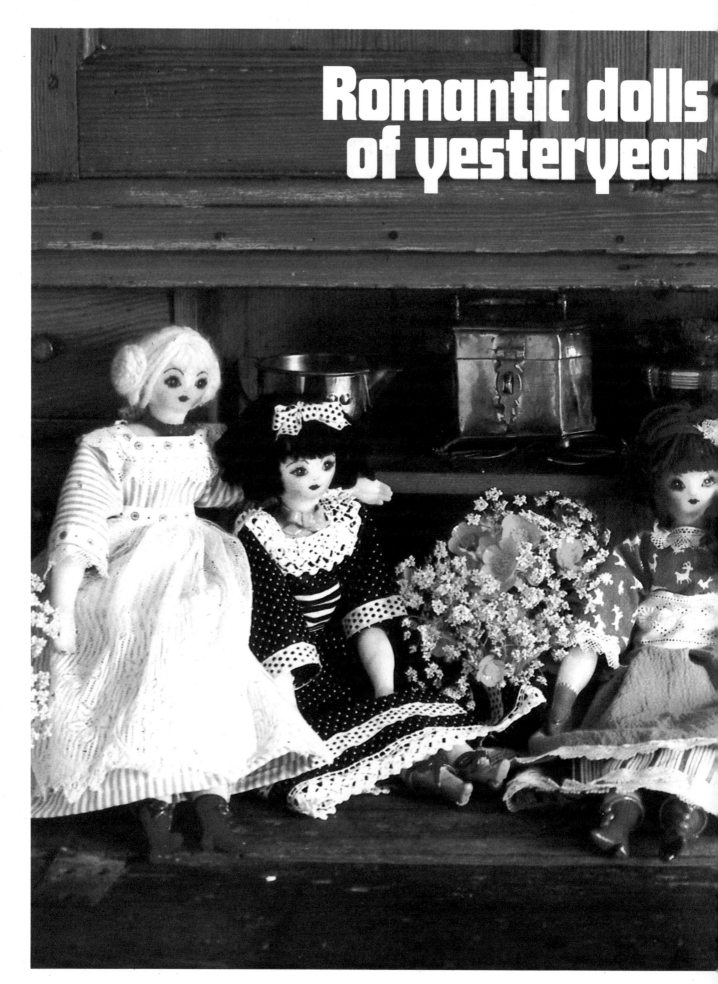

Romantic dolls of yesteryear

If you have ever admired the beautiful china dolls of the Victorian age, you will love their modern cousins, with their pale, delicate faces and their romantic clothes. They measure 38 cm (15") from the tip of their boots to their hair ribbons and have a fabric body stuffed with kapok so that they can sit up. The limbs and head are white air-setting clay which can be painted and varnished for a smooth, porcelain-like finish.

All four are made in the same way but with different clothes and hair.

Making the dolls

Materials Required: White, air-drying modelling clay. Bottle of modelling glaze. Paintbox colors. Kapok for stuffing. Small amounts of fabric, narrow elastic, lace, and yarn. 2 paint brushes (medium and fine). Wooden board. Rolling pin. Small kitchen knife.

✳

1 Warm the modelling clay slightly between your hands. For the lower arm, make a sausage 6 cm (2½") long (2 cm [¾"] diameter at top, 1 cm [⅜"] at bottom). Smooth into shape with the fingers, wetting the clay slightly if it gets too dry. Wetting it also gives a smoother finish. At the upper end, make a bulge all around to hold it in the fabric upper arm.

2 The legs are worked in the same way. In place of feet, shape small boots. For the tops of the boots and laces, roll thin pieces of clay and press them on.

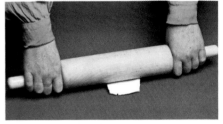

3 For the shoulder part, roll out a piece 5 cm x 8 cm (2" x 3") and about 7 mm (¼") thick with the rolling pin. Round off corners and edges.

4 With the end of the paintbrush, make holes in the 4 corners.

5 Make the neck 1 cm ($\frac{3}{8}$″) high and 2 cm ($\frac{3}{4}$″) in diameter and press onto the shoulder part. The head is then worked onto it. Make a ball about 5 cm (2″) diameter and press onto the neck. Then with knife and fingers, model the nose and smooth over the join with the neck. Try to make the head and neck as even as possible. The neckband is a thin strip of clay formed into a bow.
Finally, bend the shoulder section around to a curve.

6 Place the shaped parts on one side and leave them to set. The clay is air-setting and becomes rock-hard with a marble-like finish.

7 Now paint the various parts – the boots with laces or buttons, the hands with gloves or nails, the bow at the neck. The features on the face can be sketched in first with a pencil. If it is not right the first time, you can wipe it off again. Glaze when dry. (Glaze becomes transparent as it dries.)

9 Stuff all 5 body parts firmly with kapok. Sew the upper arms and legs to the body where indicated. Push the bulges of the clay legs and arms into the fabric legs and arms. Draw narrow tapes through the casings and knot tightly. The head-shoulder part is sewn onto the body through the 4 holes with buttonhole thread.
Cut hair from wool yarn and stick onto the head with glue; trim into shape.

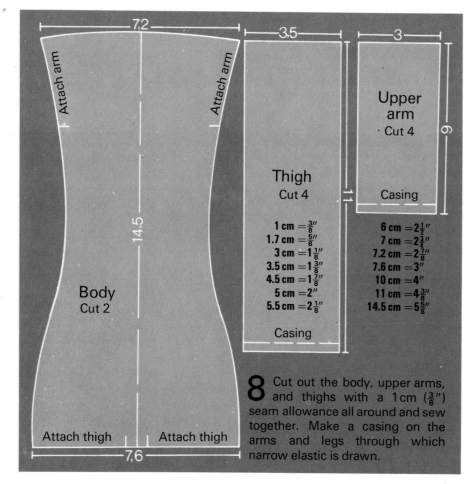

Attach arm · Attach arm

7,2

14.5

Body
Cut 2

Attach thigh · Attach thigh

7,6

3.5

Thigh
Cut 4

1 cm	= $\frac{3}{8}$″
1.7 cm	= $\frac{5}{8}$″
3 cm	= $1\frac{1}{8}$″
3.5 cm	= $1\frac{3}{8}$″
4.5 cm	= $1\frac{7}{8}$″
5 cm	= 2″
5.5 cm	= $2\frac{1}{8}$″

Casing

3

Upper arm
· Cut 4

9

Casing

11

6 cm	= $2\frac{1}{2}$″
7 cm	= $2\frac{3}{4}$″
7.2 cm	= $2\frac{7}{8}$″
7.6 cm	= 3″
10 cm	= 4″
11 cm	= $4\frac{3}{8}$″
14.5 cm	= $5\frac{5}{8}$″

8 Cut out the body, upper arms, and thighs with a 1 cm ($\frac{3}{8}$″) seam allowance all around and sew together. Make a casing on the arms and legs through which narrow elastic is drawn.

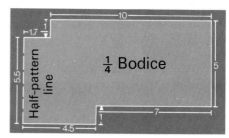

1.7 · 1 · 10

5.5 · Half-pattern line · $\frac{1}{4}$ Bodice · 5

4.5 · 1 · 7 · 1

10 Cut out the bodice of the dress twice with 1 cm ($\frac{3}{8}$″) seam allowance (it is open at the back). Join the shoulder, sleeve, and side seams. Turn in the edges of the sleeves and neck. Then cut out the skirt to measure 40 cm x 20 cm (15$\frac{3}{4}$″ x 8″) plus seam allowance and join to a circle along the narrow sides. Gather one edge and sew to the bodice; hem the other edge. This is the basic shape for all the dress variations. You can now trim the dress with lace and braid. The outfit can be completed with a little apron and a wide sash, or the dress can be made from several fabrics, as illustrated on previous pages.
Pull the dress over the doll and sew up invisibly at the back by hand.

Iron-ons just for fun

Children will love these iron-on motifs for T-shirts. Because they are built up in layers, they appear three-dimensional.

Tip the bottle and let it all run out.

These motifs have been specially designed for children and teenagers just for fun on casual clothes. To make them, you will need double-sided iron-on bonding net (available in packs) and colorful scraps of fabric. Trace the motifs onto the paper backing on the bonding net, tracing each part of the design separately. Cut around the shapes roughly and iron lightly onto the fabric. Allow the net to cool and cut out the shapes carefully. Peel off the paper backing and build up the motif by ironing on the layers under a damp cloth. Always place the largest shape at the bottom, the next size over it, and so on.

Cut out each layer individually, then iron the layers together, one on top of the other as shown above.

Wear your heart for all to see. Make it in stripes on stripes to add to the fun.

9

To build up the motifs, cut out the separate shapes in different colors and iron them one on top of the other. Take the rising sun as an example. Cut out three layers of fabric in the shape of the cloud, but in three different sizes. Iron on the blue layer first, then the purple layer, and finally the yellow one. Then cut out the orange rays and iron them on over the yellow cloud. Add the two seagulls, the semi-circular sun, and the strip of sea. The motif is now complete.

The motifs are given actual size for tracing. See what others you can invent for yourself.

11

1

2

3

4

5

6

7

Buckle down to it

Really original belt buckles are hard to find, so why not make some of your own. The buckles shown here have been cast from polyester resin with interesting objects set into them. **Style 1** shows two old photographs, **Style 3** an old print cut from a postcard. A flattened box of matches is set into **Style 2**, while a toy locomotive is used for **Style 4. Style 5** sports a favorite cartoon character and **Styles 6 and 7** contain dried and artificial flowers.
The technique for clear-cast embedding is described overleaf.

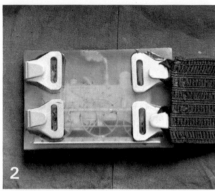

These photographs show you how to make the fastenings for the various types of buckle. For narrow buckles, glue on hooks as in photograph 1. For wider buckles, 4 hooks will be necessary as in photograph 2.

If you make a double buckle, you will need a hook and bent wire bars arranged as in photograph 3, or you can use more skirt hooks as in photograph 4.

Clear-cast embedding with polyester resin

Materials Required: Polyester resin. Hardener. Wooden stirrer. Acetone for cleaning. Non-silicone wax. Objects to embed.

Polyester resin is a transparent fluid with a consistency like syrup. When it is mixed with a hardener or catalyst, heat is generated and, on cooling, the resin is changed from a liquid to a solid state. It is therefore possible to embed all kinds of objects in the resulting clear shape — items such as coins, shells, photographs, interesting stamps, even very delicate flowers and insects.

The resin and hardener can be bought at crafts shops. Make sure that the two materials come from the same manufacturer. Complete kits are often available at crafts shops with full instructions and molds.

You will also need a piece of wood for stirring and some acetone which is useful for cleaning up spots of resin. Be careful with this as it is highly flammable. Throw away any excess when you have finished.

Special castings are available in many shapes and sizes. They are completely smooth inside so that it is only the edges and back of the molded resin that will need sanding. You can, however, use containers that you find around the home made from glass, china, tin, glazed ceramics, and enamelled metal as molds. Molds should be coated on the inside with a non-silicone wax to aid release.

Make sure that the shape of the mold does not become narrower at the top, as you will not be able to remove the cast. Also, be sure that the shape of the mold and the object to be embedded complement one another.

Making a cast

Mix the resin with the hardener and stir slowly to remove all air bubbles. Make sure that the object to be embedded is dry and dust-free. Some objects, such as dried flowers, tend to trap air, so immerse these in resin before embedding.

Polish the mold inside with the wax. Pour enough resin into the mold for the 1st layer (about half-way up). This will support the object.

Place the object upside down on the tacky surface. When this layer has dried, pour in the 2nd layer up to the top of the mold, covering the object.

If several objects are to be embedded at several levels, more layers are necessary to support the object at each level. Cover the mold with foil to keep off dust and leave until the resin has gelled. Remove the cast from the mold.

Smooth the uneven parts with coarse, then fine wet-and-dry sandpaper. Then rub all over with rubbing compound or scouring powder, finishing off with metal polish.

Safety precautions

Work in a warm, well-ventilated room on a heat-resistant surface covered with foil or waxed paper.

Keep plastics away from open flames.

Wear rubber gloves or use a barrier cream to protect your hands.

Mix the resin in disposable containers which should not be thrown away until the resin has cooled.

Any hardener spilled on the skin should be washed off immediately with cold water.

Throw away all waste materials when you have finished working.

Fastenings for the buckles

After the buckles have been cast, they will need fastenings. Use skirt hooks and wire as shown in the photographs on the left. Stick them on with epoxy glue.

Single buckles: For the narrow buckles, 1 hook on each side is sufficient (photograph 1). For the wider buckles, 2 hooks are glued on, one above the other (photograph 2). Make a belt from braided string, fabric, or leather and make loops at the ends to hook around the skirt hooks. In this way the buckle is not fastened permanently to the belt, so you can have several belts for one buckle.

Double buckles: The fastening in photograph 3 is made with 1 skirt hook and a home-made eye of strong wire. Make 2 larger bars from wire to which you fasten the belt. Bend the wire with flat-nosed pliers and twist it into a spiral at the ends to get a strong enough purchase on the glue. Stick them on as shown in the photograph. Draw the ends of the belt through the wire bars and stitch down. Another variation is shown in photograph 4.

Summer flowers for a winter bouquet

*M*ake elegant arrangements or
informal bouquets with plastic
flowers painted in soft colors and dried
grasses or evergreen leaves.

Painting plastic flowers

1 Assemble the materials above. Use enamel paint.

2 These and many other plastic flowers are available from large stores. The more varieties you use, the lovelier the bouquet will be.

3 Cut off all the leaves along the stem. Leave the sepals.

4 Each bloom needs a stem. Add wire stems if necessary.

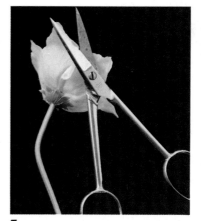

5 Trim any ragged edges of the petals with scissors.

6 Take composite flowers apart and paint each part singly.

7 Mix the colors on the plate. Pastel shades are made with large amounts of white. Paint the stems and sepals green.

For a perfect match –
pleat a hanging lampshade
from a remnant
of the wallpaper
in one of your rooms.

In the shade

An interesting old lamp base is topped with a shade made of wrapping paper.

A vase is transformed into a lamp with a shade of marbled paper.

A pleated paper lampshade is a charming accessory which will blend beautifully with a traditional or cottage setting. It is easy to make and throws a soft, flattering light.

Materials Required: A lamp base, bottle, or vase with electric light fitting or a hanging light fixture. Wire lampshade frame in size and shape suitable for the base. Paper (not too thick, otherwise the light will not shine through) such as wrapping paper, wallpaper, marbled book end paper. Ribbon or cord. Glue. Hole punch.

Making the shade

1 Cut the paper so that it overlaps the lower edge of the frame by about 1 cm ($\frac{3}{8}$") and the upper edge by 2 cm–3 cm ($\frac{3}{4}$"–1$\frac{1}{4}$"). If you wish to cut a zigzag edge, make sure that the lower or upper ring is still covered. The length should be 2–2$\frac{1}{2}$ times as long as the circumference of the lower frame ring. Stick several strips of paper together to make up the length if necessary. On one short side, add 1 cm ($\frac{3}{8}$") extra for gluing the shade together. Now draw in the pleat lines. The width of the pleats should be 2 cm–3 cm ($\frac{3}{4}$"–1$\frac{1}{4}$"), but only the inner pleat lines are marked, ie. on a 3 cm (1$\frac{1}{4}$") pleat, space the lines 6 cm (2$\frac{1}{2}$") apart. Pleat line after line, pinching the pleats firmly.

2 + 3 Now the holes for the cord are punched in about 1 cm ($\frac{3}{8}$") from the inside folds and 4 cm–6 cm (1$\frac{1}{2}$"–2$\frac{1}{2}$") from the upper edge, according to the height of the shade. Use a punch for this or, alternatively, pierce the holes with a needle first and then with a knitting needle. To fix the shade onto the frame, punch half holes on the inside pleats, halfway between the upper edge and the cord holes (photograph 3). You can also cut small notches.

4 If you do not want to leave the upper or lower edges straight, cut them to the desired zigzag shape. Cut each pleat separately, otherwise the effect will be uneven. Glue the side edge to the 1 cm ($\frac{3}{8}$") allowance and leave to dry. Draw the cord or ribbon through the holes. Place the shade onto the frame so that the half holes fit onto the upper ring and draw up the cord. Tie the cord into a knot or bow.

5 + 6 To make a lamp from a bottle or vase, you will have to buy a special light fitting which can be inserted into the opening.

First, pleat the paper.

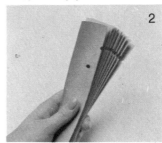

Punch in holes for cord . . .

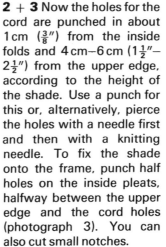

. . . and half holes for upper ring.

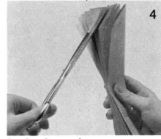

Cut the edges to shape.

For a vase or bottle . . .

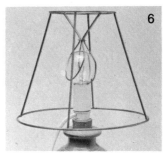

. . . add a special light fitting.

New
looks
for
books

Protect your recipe books
from kitchen splashes
and stains with a smart
new cover in vinyl-coated cloth.

Notebooks, address books, recipe books, diaries, albums – all those books which are in constant use will benefit from a strong, protective covering. Or you may want to give your favorite book an attractive face-lift, or make a very individual present.

Books which suffer a lot of wear and tear, such as the recipe books shown in the large photograph, will last longer if they are bound in vinyl-coated cloth. They will look brighter and can simply be wiped clean.

The selection of books on the right have been covered in different ways to suit their contents. Here we left the spines free and covered only the front and back surfaces. All kinds of materials can be used – a beautiful fabric, a photograph, an art postcard, a favorite picture from a magazine.

It is very important to work neatly for a professional finish. Use a metal ruler and sharp craft knife for cutting. If using fabric, turn in edges to stop fraying. On rounded corners snip fabric several times so that it lies flat. Whatever you use as a cover, stick it on with a good adhesive.

Many materials such as magazine illustrations, wallpaper, printed fabrics, and old photographs can be used to cover your books.

1 Draw the outlines of the book onto the wrong side of the fabric and mark the width of the spine.

2 Cut the fabric around the shape, adding 1 cm ($\frac{3}{8}$″) extra all around. Cut wedges on either side of the spine.

3 Apply fabric adhesive thinly onto one outside cover. Place the book onto the fabric and press down firmly.

4 Apply adhesive to the book spine and turn the tabs to the inside. Press on the fabric. Glue the other side.

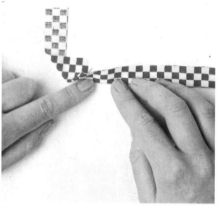

5 Turn the excess fabric to the inside of the cover and glue in place. Miter the corners neatly.

6 To make the book look neat from the inside, paste the first and last pages over the edges of the fabric.

Salad days

Our picnic case holds everything that you will need for a carefree "al fresco" meal.

An ordinary fiber-board suitcase can be transformed into a smart picnic case. It is sturdy, and roomy enough to accommodate your knives and forks, thermos, plates, and glasses as well as the food. It is also well-insulated and has a compartment to hold ice packs which will keep the food cool.

Size: The inside measurements of the case illustrated are 25 cm x 42 cm (10" x 16½"), 11 cm (4½") deep, with a 3.5 cm (1½") deep lid. This is large enough for a picnic for three people. The same technique can be used for a picnic case of any size.

Materials Required: Paint in a can or aerosol. Vinyl-coated fabric: 1.50 m (1⅝ yds), 100 cm (39") wide. Cardboard to fit base, sides, and lid. Sheets of expanded polystyrene, 1 cm (⅜") thick to fit base, lid, and sides. Glue. About 70 upholsterers' tacks or studs. 2 punch-in press studs or snaps. Craft knife. Tenon saw. Piece of plywood, 6 mm (¼") thick, to fit inside the case.

1 The case is painted first, either with a brush or a spray. Cover the handle, locks, and corners with masking tape before you begin. Paint the case several times (at least three times if using spray paint). Keep moving the can while spray-painting, first from top to bottom, then from left to right. Leave the paint to dry well between coats.

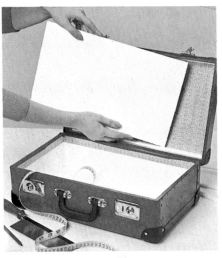

2 The case is lined with poly-styrene to insulate it. Measure the base, lid, and sides, and cut out pieces to fit with a tenon saw, making the sides shorter than the case sides. Move the saw with a pulling motion only to avoid cracking the poly-styrene. First glue the side strips lightly and insert into the case. Then fit the lid and base sheets in tightly. Now measure the base and sides again and draw the areas onto the cardboard, extending the sides out from the base. Cut out with a craft knife against a metal ruler. All around the base, score lightly along the lines to enable you to bend up the sides (see the cardboard in the photograph below). Draw and cut out the lid in the same way.

3 Then place both base and lid patterns onto the wrong side of the vinyl-coated fabric and cut out with a 2 cm (¾") seam allowance all around. At the corners, either snip into the fabric or cut across diagonally. Then coat the outer edges of the cardboard base and lid with glue (the sides are glued later). Also apply glue to the same areas on the wrong side of the fabric. Leave to dry slightly for about 10–15 minutes, then place the surfaces together precisely. Press together well, making sure that no wrinkles form.

Now glue the sides in the same way, making sure that no wrinkles form. Then, the 2 cm ($\frac{3}{4}$″) wide allowances are glued down. Here also, both the fabric and the edge of the paper are covered with glue.

Finally, fold the sides into a box shape.

4 The fabric-lined box shape should fit tightly into the case covering the polystyrene strips. The same applies to the lid with its narrower sides. Push them firmly into place.

5 The case is then divided into three sections: for glasses, for a thermos flask, and for the food compartment. Cut out two pieces of cardboard to fit and glue fabric onto both sides, leaving 2 cm ($\frac{3}{4}$″) over at each end.

Slot the divisions into the case, turning the ends back with paper clips. Then apply glue to these ends and to adjacent sides of the case, and glue together.

6 We made a tray from the sheet of plywood, which also serves as a dividing lid during transport. At the narrow ends, saw out grip-holes with a tenon saw and sand all edges. The surfaces can be covered in vinyl-coated fabric or adhesive plastic in a matching color.

Plates and knives and forks are held in two pockets in the lid, each measuring 21 cm x 18 cm (8$\frac{1}{4}$″ x 7″). Make yours to fit your own case.

7 Plate pocket: Draw the required shape onto cardboard, then cut out and round off the two upper corners. Glue the cardboard onto the wrong side of a large piece of fabric. At each side, draw an equal-sided triangle on the fabric. The upper edge should be 8 cm (3″) long; the triangle points downwards.

Cut out the pocket, adding 2 cm ($\frac{3}{4}$″) at the sides and bottom. Cut out the entire pocket once more in fabric and glue to the first pocket shape. The

added allowances are turned in and glued to the lid of the case.

Then glue 2 strips of fabric together and cut out a tab measuring 11 cm x 6 cm (4$\frac{1}{2}$″ x 2$\frac{1}{2}$″) and another piece measuring 4 cm x 6 cm (1$\frac{1}{2}$″ x 2$\frac{1}{2}$″). Round off the corners. Punch the halves of a press stud or snap into the two parts. Glue the tab to the inside of the pocket with an underlap of 4 cm (1$\frac{1}{2}$″); glue the other part onto the lid. The plates fit neatly into this pocket, which opens out as shown in the photograph.

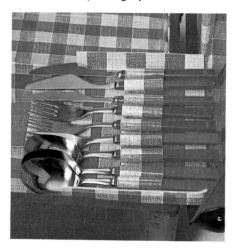

8 The knife and fork pocket is the same size as the plate pocket with rounded edges, but it has 3 cm (1$\frac{1}{4}$″) walls on the sides and bottom. Cut the shape in cardboard and glue fabric onto both sides. The bottom wall is glued onto the lid side. Make the tab parts as for the plate compartment. To hold the knives and forks in place, stitch a 4 cm (1$\frac{1}{2}$″) wide strip of double fabric in loops onto another strip, then glue this to the inside of the pocket.

9 Fasten the base and lid inserts onto the frame with the tacks or studs; if possible, fasten the two pockets to the lid in the same way.

Sweet wagon　　　　　**Stick wagon**　　　　　**Lollipop wagon**

What an ambush! A train-load of delicious sweets!

A party train in cardboard

Ambush on the Candy Express!

Partytime is time to have fun and to eat lots of brightly-colored sweets. What better way of delivering the goodies than on the Candy Express with its sturdy locomotive and gay wagons full to the brim of tantalizing treats! It's simple to make from strong cardboard and will stand up to a lot of wear and tear on the day of the party. The children can each take home a wagon filled with booty, and when all the sweets have been eaten, the wagons can become boxes for storing small treasures.

Materials Required: Heavy cardboard. Craft knife. Poster paints. Quick-setting glue. Clear varnish.

Making the train
The parts of the locomotive and wagons are given on the graph overleaf. Enlarge them on a grid drawn directly onto the cardboard. Four of the wagons are exactly the same size; the only way they differ is in the cutting out of the sides and the painting. The exception is the stick wagon, which has only two low sides and no back or front.

When the outlines have been drawn on the cardboard, cut along the outlines with the craft knife held against a metal ruler to ensure a straight edge. Uneven edges can be smoothed with fine sandpaper.

After cutting out all the parts of the train, paint them in the colors and patterns shown on the graph.

Wagons: When the paint is dry, glue the sides of each wagon to the edges of the base (not on top of it). Then stick the front and back to the base between the side pieces. Add the strips along the top edge of the sides.

Bonbon wagon   Licorice wagon   Locomotive

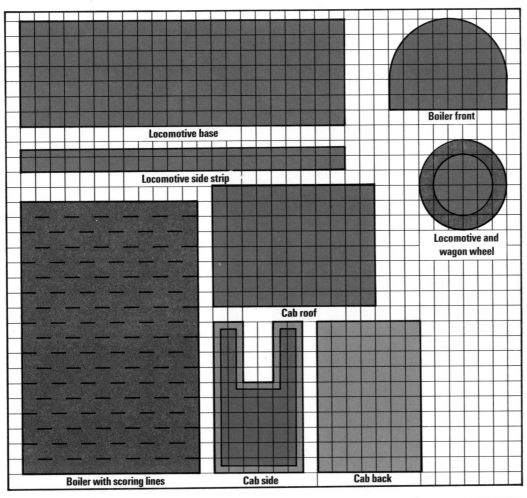

Locomotive base

Boiler front

Locomotive side strip

Locomotive and wagon wheel

Cab roof

Boiler with scoring lines

Cab side

Cab back

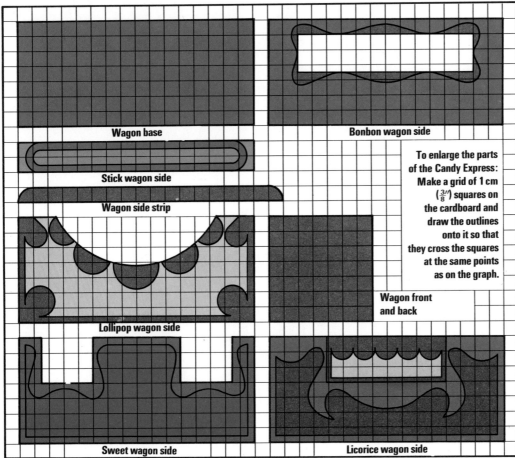

Wagon base

Bonbon wagon side

Stick wagon side

Wagon side strip

To enlarge the parts of the Candy Express: Make a grid of 1 cm ($\frac{3}{8}''$) squares on the cardboard and draw the outlines onto it so that they cross the squares at the same points as on the graph.

Wagon front and back

Lollipop wagon side

Sweet wagon side

Licorice wagon side

If you want the wheels to turn, pin them on with glass-headed pins; otherwise, glue them to the sides.

Finally, coat the wagons with clear varnish to make the surface smooth.

Locomotive: The locomotive is slightly more complicated to make. First glue the narrow side strips to the long edges of the base. Score the boiler along the lines marked on the graph pattern, bend it around to a cylindrical shape, and glue it to the top edges of the side strips, 2 cm ($\frac{3}{4}''$) from the front. Then glue on the front of the boiler, shaping it to fit with sandpaper.

Glue the sides of the driver's cab immediately behind the boiler, then add the back of the cab between the sides. Stick on the roof so that it protrudes 2 cm ($\frac{3}{4}''$) over the boiler in the front. Position the wheels as follows: The back ones go directly under the center of the cab, the others are placed at 6 cm ($2\frac{3}{8}''$) intervals.

Coat the locomotive with clear varnish as for the wagons.

If you wish to make couplings so that the locomotive will pull the wagons, cut out strips measuring 1 cm x 6 cm ($\frac{3}{8}''$ x $2\frac{1}{4}''$) and fasten them with short pins to the underside of the wagons and locomotive. The train is now ready for action!

Making a wooden train

For a more substantial toy, the train can also be made of plywood with firm axles for the wheels. Cut out the shapes with an ordinary tenon saw, and the windows in the wagons and the wheels with a fret saw. Glue the parts together; paint and varnish them as for the cardboard train (for extra strength, use wood glue).

A cut above the others

Transform any plain surface into a riot of color with the art of découpage. The designs are made up of a number of cut-out shapes which are then pasted down, varnished, and sandpapered until the paper is embedded in the layers of varnish and a beautifully smooth surface appears. We have decorated everyday objects such as a tray, a pillbox, a tea caddy, a face-cream jar, and other small boxes.

6

7

We have used one of the examples from the previous pages to illustrate the technique of découpage.

Materials Required: Tin or plastic container or tray. Wet-and-dry sandpaper. Colored spray paint. Small, sharp scissors. Paper paste or glue. Colored prints or magazine illustrations. Brush and clear varnish.

First sandpaper the article thoroughly and spray with paint. Then decide on the theme for the decoration and choose the prints or the magazine illustrations.

Cut them out very precisely, carefully cutting close to the flower petals and stems and taking care not to cut right through any fine lines. Cut larger motifs according to the size of the item you are covering. Alternatively, cut out smaller motifs to be grouped as a larger motif. Arrange the motifs, moving them around until the most pleasing pattern is formed before sticking them down. Take your time over this preliminary planning. Don't start until the design is planned.

If using magazine illustrations, test-glue a scrap to be sure the printing on the other side of the paper won't show through.

Now spread paste on the underside of the motifs one by one, working on a sheet of paper. You need to change the work surface often to prevent the face of the scraps from sticking to it and tearing as you lift them off.

Always stick on the motifs from the outside to the inside or, on larger surfaces, from one side to the other. If you want the base color to show, arrange the motifs with spaces between. Otherwise, make a solid cover by placing them so that they overlap slightly.

Stick an especially attractive motif over the final space. Make sure that the paste has reached right to the edge of the motifs. Test them afterward and, if necessary, spread some more paste under the edges. Remove any paste stains with a damp cloth. Any torn areas can be touched up with a felt-tipped pen.

Finally, coat the whole surface with a colorless varnish. Leave to dry thoroughly and then sandpaper it. Repeat the varnishing and sanding process, building up layers of varnish until a completely smooth and hard-wearing surface is achieved.

Everyone loves strolling along the beach in the summer, picking up beautiful, pearly shells. Most people can't bear to part with them, so they take a whole bagful home as a souvenir, only to put them in a corner and forget all about them. However, you can keep your happy summer memories alive by decorating objects around the house with the shells. Choose the colors and shapes with care and you'll achieve very pleasing results with far more charm than the average pieces of shellcraft sold in souvenir shops.

First, decide what you want to decorate, a mirror frame or a little trinket box for example, then sort the shells into groups of the same type. Play around with the different patterns they will make; the long, spiral shells look attractive radiating from a central point, while the small, fanlike shells make a pretty scalloped edge or the petals of a flower. Larger shells can be added here and there for variety. Glue them to the surface with clear glue. If desired, varnish them when dry.

Seaside souvenirs

Decorate a wooden box with shells. Before gluing them on, paint the box in a neutral background color.

Try a baroque effect for an old mirror frame with assorted seashells.

Pick of the bunch

Our impressive floral centerpiece will never wither or fade as the "flowers" are made of painted pine cones interspersed with a variety of dried grasses, seed heads, thistles, and evergreen leaves.

Materials Required:

Container. Polystyrene to fill container. Glue. Poster paint in white and a variety of colors. Clear varnish. Pine cones. Cutters to halve pine cones. Small seeds, dried seed heads, grasses, thistles. Absorbent cotton balls. Wooden kebab sticks.

Making the bouquet

Choose a suitable container. You may wish to use a basket, earthenware pot, or brass bowl (the latter must be painted with a thin coat of varnish to avoid tarnishing). Fill the container with layers of polystyrene cut to size (photograph 1) and glue it down around the edge. Paint the surface of the top layer in a dark color (see photograph 6). For the flowers, you will need some well-dried pine cones. Halve these across the center with cutters (photograph 2). The lower, wide part is used for the flowers. Drill a hole through from the bottom and insert a painted wooden kebab stick as a stem. Glue firmly. Dip the flowers into thinned white paint and leave to dry well. Then dip them into colored paint, mixed as desired (photograph 3). If a cone closes up again after painting, put it into the oven to dry it out until it reopens.

Cover the center of each flower with glue and sprinkle it with small seeds. Alternatively, paint it in a contrasting color. Finally, spray some of the flowers lightly with clear varnish, leaving others matt for contrast (photograph 4).

When making up the bouquet, work from the center outwards, positioning the center flowers higher than the surrounding ones for a well-balanced effect.

Fill in the spaces with dried seed heads, dried grasses, and thistles. You can also glue small balls of absorbent cotton onto kebab sticks, dip them into paint, and decorate with small acorns or cloves (photograph 5). Or cover with glue and dip into poppy seeds or mustard seeds. Another idea is to halve larger balls of cotton and glue dried peas onto them.

For the finishing touch, add green or dark red evergreens to the bouquet, placing them among light-colored dried flowers.

1 First choose a suitable container such as a brass bowl and line it with layers of polystyrene cut to fit the shape exactly.

2 For the flowers, you will need the lower halves of some well-dried pine cones. Cut them through the center.

3 Stick the flower shape onto a painted kebab stick and dip into thinned white paint. When dry, dip into colored paint.

4 To add interest to the bouquet, spray some of the flowers with a clear varnish, leaving others matt.

5 Other decorations include cotton balls glued onto kebab sticks and dipped into poppy or mustard seeds.

6 When arranging the bouquet, work from the center toward the outside, with the central ones higher than the rest.

All things bright and beautiful

Take a box of lovely shiny beads and see what your imagination can do with them. Threading them up to make these eye-catching belts is child's play and the belts are wonderful accessories for casual outfits that need that special something to lift them out of the ordinary. For the flat belt (top), pick up 5 beads for each row. At one end, leave a loose bead loop to hook the fastening into. The buckle is sewn to the other end. For the tube belt, pick up 8 beads in each round.

Materials Required:

Medium to fine beads in various colors. Fine beading needle. Synthetic thread (use double). Buckle which will hook into end of belt.

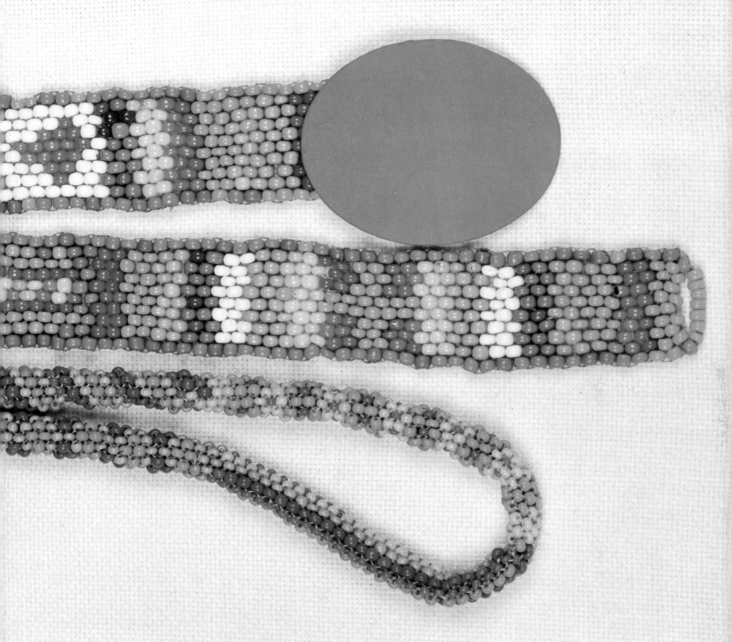

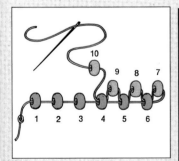

1 Thread the needle with as long a thread as possible and string the beads according to the width of the belt. For our example, we have used 6 beads in each row. After the 7th bead, take the thread back through the 6th, then pick up the 8th, go back through the 5th, and so on until 6 beads are threaded in the 2nd row.

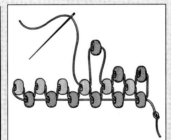

2 After the 2nd row, turn the work and thread the 3rd row in the same way. The beads never rest on top of one another, but fit neatly in between those of the row before.

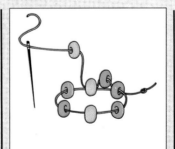

3 For the bead tube, pick up the beads and join into a circle by threading through the first bead again. For the 2nd round, pick up a bead, thread through the 2nd bead, pick up another bead and so on. If you have difficulty distinguishing between rounds (difficult with small beads) take a new color for every round.

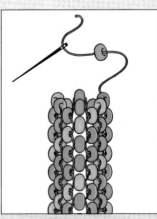

4 To create a spiral pattern, thread each bead of each successive round to match the bead just below it. To finish off, add more beads to the round to form a knot and make bead fringes.

Make the most of a slim waist with a bead belt. The technique is simple and you can choose your own colors.

Bead beautiful

Pattern Diagram ▶

1

2

Materials Required (for a belt about 68–76 cm [$26\frac{3}{4}$–30"] long): Rocaille beads No. 10 in the following colors and approximate quantities (approx. $\frac{1}{2}$ oz per box): 9 boxes dark blue, 1 box each white, yellow, red, green, and pale blue. 5 beads with 1 cm ($\frac{3}{8}$") diameter. Fine transparent synthetic yarn (used double). Fine sewing needle.

Making the belt

In the 1st row, secure the 1st bead well, then thread 41 beads in the main color. Then count back 10 beads and take the thread through the next bead along. Then pick up 5 beads and go through the 6th bead back along the row (see Diagram 1). Pick up 5 more beads and again go through the 6th bead back along the row. Repeat to end of row. Turn the work and hold it between the 1st finger and thumb of your left hand with the thread on the right. In the 3rd and all remaining rows, always pick up 5 beads and insert the needle through the 3rd bead of a loop. After 6 loops, turn. Work the colored diamond pattern as shown on the diagram. The number of diamonds you require will be determined by your waist measurement. Work at least 3 rows in the main color before 1st and after last diamond. To make the fastening, thread 10 beads instead of 5 in the last row. Sew the 5 large beads to the other end of the belt.

◀ Diagrams 1 and 2 show how simple the technique is. The bead loops consist of 5 beads and the needle is always inserted into the 3rd bead of the loop below. On the Pattern Diagram, you can see how the diamonds are worked into the loop pattern of each row.

String it all together

Thread a few beads here, a tassel or two there, and in no time you'll have a set of lovely belts. Decorate a long dress or wrap one around a scarf.

<u>Size:</u> Each belt is about 1.95 m (2⅛ yds) long.

<u>Materials Required:</u> (for each belt) 7 skeins of embroidery yarn in various colors. 64 wooden beads, 1 cm (⅜") diameter. 20 wooden beads, 0.7 cm (¼") diameter. 2 large oval or bell-shaped beads. Narrow cotton braid. Crochet cotton for threading beads.

Making the belt

If your skeins of embroidery yarn are not ready-twisted, unwind 5 of them. Rewind each separately around a piece of cardboard 32 cm (12½") long. Slip off cardboard. Hold ends taut, twist in opposite directions, and when tight, thread one end through the other. The skein will twist automatically. Wrap braid round the skeins 2 cm (¾") from ends and stitch down.

Sew 12 cm (4¾") lengths of crochet cotton into braid and knot together at the skein. Knot a small bead onto each end.

Thread beads between skeins as follows: draw a 30 cm (11¾") length of crochet cotton through the end of a skein and knot close to the skein. Thread 8 large beads onto each of the strands, knot the strands together, and draw ends through the next skein. Knot strands together well and cut threads. Repeat 4 times in all.

At ends of 2 outer skeins, thread a larger oval or bell-shaped bead. For the tassels, cut 2 different-colored skeins in half and place half of each together. Knot them onto ends of belt and wrap braid around the top to secure.

Something fishy.....

Here's a really original idea for some summer necklaces. The lovely, shiny fish are, in fact, lures from specialist fishing tackle shops. Hung from a chain of matching beads they are the perfect fun accessory for T-shirts and swimsuits. Besides the lures, you will need the following materials: nylon thread, necklace fastenings, small round beads, and bugle beads in matching colors, a small pair of pliers. First, cut off the fish hook with the pliers. Then measure out a piece of nylon thread to the desired length. Position the lure in the center and knot it, then thread the beads. The necklace will look prettiest if you choose beads to pick up the colors in the lures. Knot the fastenings onto the ends and pass the thread back through the last beads. For extra security, you can melt the ends of the thread very carefully over a flame. Longer necklaces do not require a fastening as they will pass straight over your head.

Materials Required:
Selection of colored, fla
sequins. Elastic thread.
Fastenings such as
jump ring and bolt ring.

The sequins required
are thin and flat. They
are available in a range
of colors and diameters
so you can make
chokers of varying
thicknesses. Choose
colors that tone with
one another such as
shades of pink and
mauve, or pick strong
contrasting colors such
as red, white, and
black. Then decide the
order of threading. Mos
effective are long bands
of one color
interspersed with short
stripes of several other
colors. The selection on
the left should give you
plenty of ideas.
The chokers look
marvellous with plain
summer T-shirts and,
worn in groups of five
or six, have the impact
of beautiful tribal
necklaces. Making them
is very simple — all you
do is thread the sequins
onto elastic thread and
finish off the ends with
a fastening. You can
also make attractive
longer necklaces by
doubling the
quantity of sequins.

Threaded with sequins

Exotic origins

Necklaces can be made from practically anything — all that's needed is a little ingenuity. Here's one idea to start you experimenting. Sequins are threaded onto elastic thread to make colorful chokers which can be worn singly or one above the other.

Baubles and bangles from shiny beads

Make striking abstract and geometric designs with a variety of rich bead colors.

Experiment with the effects produced by mixing transparent and opaque colors.

Beading is a satisfying way to use your creative talents to make accessories for yourself or gifts for your friends! You can make all sorts of things from bracelets, necklaces, and pendants to purses, watch straps, glasses cases, and even small pictures! Large wooden beads can be woven into belts, table mats, or napkin rings, using the same technique. Bead weaving appeals to all ages, and even children can join in the fun. You will find that large wooden beads are the easiest for them to handle.

Materials Required:

Beads: These can be obtained in a wide variety of shapes, sizes, and colors. They can be made of glass, plastic, wood, or clay. Always use beads of the same size in bead weaving.
Beading needle: This is a long, thin needle designed to thread through tiny seed beads such as the ones shown on these pages.
Thread: Beading thread.
Findings: for bracelets and necklaces.

Planning the design

The designs shown here are intended as ideas to start your imagination working. You can copy them from the photographs or plan your own on squared paper. However, you may prefer to work with the beads rather than a sketch. Line a box with felt or an adhesive surface and arrange the beads in a pleasing design. The lining will prevent the beads from jumping about as you pick them up on the needle.

Working the design

Following the directions for flat beading or tubular chains, work the pieces according to the desired pattern or design. You may find it easier to practise at first with just two colors. You will be surprised by the number of two-color designs you can make.

Finishing the piece

Attach the findings as shown in the bead weaving directions.

If a continuous flat piece or tube is being made without metal findings, run the thread from each end into the rows at the other end. Secure the thread with a knot between two beads. Cut thread close to knot.

Making fringe

Bead fringe is a pretty way to finish pendants. After working the last row, pick up a number of beads on the thread and run it back through the last bead in the previous row. Repeat for each bead in the last row. When you have finished the fringe, run the thread back through several rows and knot the end between two beads. Cut thread close to knot.

Stitch beads to a covered button and make an interesting, uneven surface with beads of many different sizes.

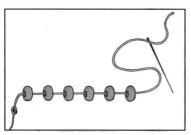

Hold the work between your thumb and forefinger.

Bead weaving: without a loom

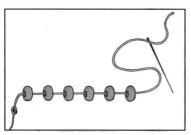

1 Flat beading: Thread beading needle with a length of thread as long as possible and tie a knot in one end. Pick up 6 beads.

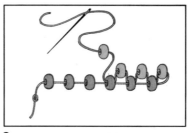

2 Pick up bead 7 and thread back through bead 6. Pick up bead 8 and thread back through bead 5. Work 6 beads in row 2.

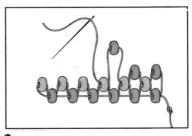

3 Continue to work rows of 6 beads added between the beads of the previous row until you have used up the thread.

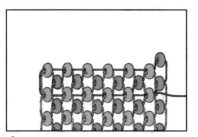

4 When the thread is almost used up, run the end back through the beads in several rows and tie a knot.

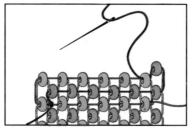

5 Knot in a new thread between two beads, and run the thread through the rows to the point where you left off.

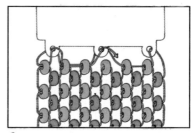

6 To attach the findings, run the thread through the holes in the findings and through the beads. Knot the thread ends.

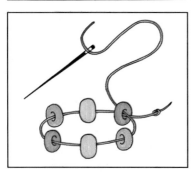

7 Tubular chain: Thread a bead needle with a length of thread as long as possible and tie a knot in one end. Pick up 6 beads and make a ring by threading through bead 1 again. A larger tube can be made by using more beads in each round.

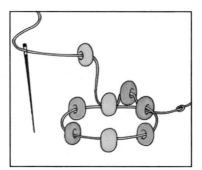

8 Continue to work the rounds by adding beads between the beads of the previous round. Begin and end threads as for flat pieces. It is difficult to distinguish between rounds with small beads, so you may wish to practice with stripes.

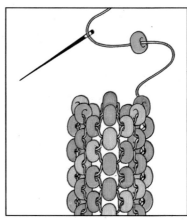

9 Spiral patterns and diagonal lines: Repeat the color of the bead you are threading through in the previous row or round.

A bead curtain to let in fresh air

A bead curtain is marvelous for summer. Hang it in the doorway to your garden or balcony and it will allow the air to circulate while keeping the flies out. Or use it indoors to partition rooms with a bold splash of color. Our bead curtain has a design of stylized birds and leaves. The pattern is created by threading the beads of different colors onto lengths of string over an actual-size drawing. It's a simple technique and even children will love to try it.

The method of working the bead curtain is explained overleaf.

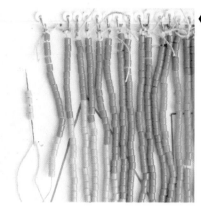

The lengths of fine string are knotted onto the runners or hooks. The beads are threaded with a needle, following the design which lies underneath. Try to keep the shapes as near as possible to the pattern.

For a good overall impression as the curtain progresses, work only 50 cm (19½″) at a time.
After threading each group of strings, hold them together in bundles, winding the strings around a nail.

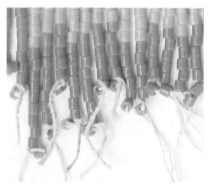

Secure the strands by bringing up each string and tying a knot between the last bead and the bead before it.

Here is a detail of the curtain showing part of a bird's head. The strands should lie close together during the work.

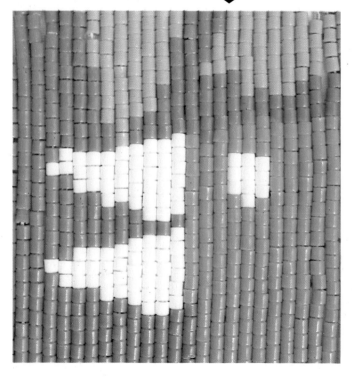

Size: When pushed closely together, the bead curtain measures 2.10 m (2¼ yd) long by 48 cm (19″) wide. If it is hung loosely, it will cover a doorway measuring 70 cm (27½″) wide. For a closer pattern or for a wider doorway, just add a few more rows of background.

Materials Required: Curtain rail measuring the same as width of the doorway. Curtain runners or hooks. Strong, fine string. Large-eyed needle. A few long nails. Cylindrical porcelain beads in dark blue, medium blue, pale green, and white.

Making the curtain

Enlarge the design from the graph pattern. The actual-size pattern will lie underneath the strings for a guide as you work. The curtain is most easily worked on a large piece of board or on the floor. Spread out the pattern and fasten the curtain rail at the top end with a few nails so that it does not shift.

Cut the string into lengths which measure the same as the height of the doorway, adding about 30 cm (12″) for the knots at beginning and end. Fasten the strings to the runners or hooks with double knots, then slide them onto the curtain rail and attach stoppers at either end. To prevent the strings from getting tangled as you work, divide them into small groups and wind the ends round a nail when you are not using them (see the second picture on the left). The runners or hooks should be up against one another as you thread the beads.

Beginning at one side, take one string from the first group and thread the beads according to the pattern underneath until the string of beads is 50 cm (19½″) long. Keep pushing the beads firmly upward. Work strand after strand of the first group in this way. Then wind the strings back around the nail. Continue threading beads onto all the strings of the other groups until each strand of beads is 50 cm (19½″). Thread a further 50 cm (19½″) on each string and continue in this way until the whole curtain length has been completed. As you work, keep comparing the strands of beads with the design.

When all the beads are in place, push the beads on each strand firmly upward. Bring each string up and tie a secure knot between the last bead and the bead before it, as shown in the third picture, left. Do not cut off the string at the bottom of the strands immediately. When the curtain has been hanging up for a while, the string will stretch slightly and then you can make any necessary adjustments.

To keep the strands equidistant, knot the runners or hooks together at 1 cm (⅜″) intervals.

The curtain rail can be painted so that it blends in with the door frame.

Enlarge your pattern for the bead curtain from the graph on page 45. Divide a large piece of paper, measuring about 2.10 m (2¼ yd) long by 0.5 m (½ yd) wide, into 12 cm (4¾″) squares. Draw the outlines of the design onto the paper, so that they cross the squares in the same places as on the graph pattern.

Cutting comments

Block printing is a wonderful way to make your own fabric designs. We've printed fabric for a tablecloth and cushions to illustrate the technique. The designs are given opposite. Enlarge them onto graph paper with 0.5 cm ($\frac{1}{4}$") squares. The size of our tablecloth is 128 cm (50$\frac{1}{2}$") square. We printed the edge with the rectangular pattern, the inner area with rows of the three square patterns. The cushion covers are 41 cm (16") square.

Materials Required:
Linoleum. Linoleum cutting set: handle and blades. Rubber roller. Sheet of glass or plastic for inking slab. Fabric. Fabric paints. Methylated spirits for cleaning the printing block and roller. Pieces of wood as a base for the linoleum. Craft knife. Paint brush. White crayon. Pencil. Ruler.
Linoleum: Use the specially prepared blocks available in craft shops or ordinary floor linoleum.
Paint: Use special fabric-printing paints or dyes, available from art and craft shops. They come in a wide range of colors.
Fabric: We used cotton for the tablecloth and cushions. You can, however, print on any closely-woven fabric made of natural fibres. Lino printing is not suitable for roughly-woven fabrics. Fabrics with a lot of sizing or dressing should be washed before use, otherwise the color may be washed out with the fabric finish. Wash the whole length of fabric before you begin and cut out only after printing.

Transferring the design:
Tape the design onto the linoleum with dressmaker's carbon paper in between. Trace all the lines with a pencil.

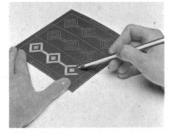

Lift off the paper and cut the linoleum to the proper size with the craft knife. With a white pencil fill in the parts that are to be printed as it is easy to make mistakes when cutting.

Cutting out: Cut around the design outlines with

the finest blade — but do not cut into backing.

Cut out the areas not to be printed with a blade of the relevant width (never cut toward your other hand!). Correct any unevenness with the fine blade. Now glue the finished piece onto a wooden block, the same size as the linoleum to enable you to see the edges when printing.

Printing: Squeeze a little paint onto the inking slab. Spread evenly with roller.

Now roll the paint evenly over the block.

Make a few test prints to make sure the color is not too faint or too strong, then begin the actual printing. The best place is on the floor on a thick layer of newspapers. The paper must lie flat, as every crease will be visible in the print. Place the block flat onto the fabric. To exert a maximum pressure, stand on the block for about 30 seconds, then get off carefully. Alternatively, tap the back of the block all over with a wooden mallet. Roll on more paint and continue to print. Correct any unevenness in the pattern with a paint brush.
The fabric must now be left to dry, for several days if necessary. When the fabric is completely dry, iron it (usually on the reverse side, but check with the paint manufacturer's instructions) with a hot iron. This fixes the color fast to the fabric and the print is then washable.
Finally, cut the fabric out to the correct size. Hem the tablecloth. Sew up 3 sides of the cushion covers and insert zipper in 4th side.

Print each cushion with a different pattern to practice the technique.

The tablecloth has been printed with the square designs in the center and the rectangular pattern as an edging. The cushions have been printed with only one design on each. The paints also come in a range of lovely colors.

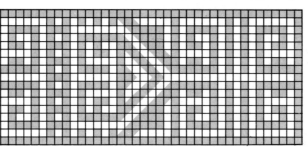

Here are the designs for the linoleum blocks given in a reduced form. Enlarge the motifs onto graph paper with 0.5 cm ($\frac{1}{4}''$) squares to give you the actual-size design. The filled-in squares show the printed area; the white ones are cut out.

 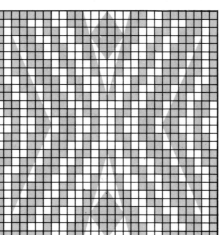 

Potato printing on tablecloths, place mats, napkins

Color and imagination are all you need

Colored butterflies decorate this party tablecloth. They are printed along the hem as a border and in a circle in the center. Use many colors for the wings.

▲ Two rows of apples edge the place mat. A subtle effect is produced by using a stamp several times without dipping it in the paint.

◀ Print place cards with the same motif as the tablecloth.

Potato printing is an effective way of making pretty designs from simple shapes. The most obvious shapes to work with are straight-sided geometric ones such as squares, rectangles, triangles, stars, or bars. But with a little more care you can cut round or oval motifs into the potatoes. The effect is created by the regular repetition of the shapes, which can be placed on top of or beside each other.

51

Choosing the materials

To make the stamps, choose large potatoes which are really firm and fresh. You can print onto most kinds of fabric and paper. The most suitable fabric for a tablecloth is cotton or a cotton/linen blend. Coarse weaves or very textured fabrics will distort the design. Fabric with dressing or sizing on it should be washed before being printed because part of the color will dissolve along with the dressing or sizing at the first wash and the design will become fuzzy at the edges.

Cover the working surface with a plastic cloth or a large clean sheet of paper.

For the stamp pad, stretch a piece of felt over half the area of a wooden board; the other half can be used as a cutting board for the potatoes.

Arranging motifs

Potato printing is especially decorative on place mats, napkins, tablecloths and runners, curtains, or cards, where the motif appears several times. In repeat patterns — where the motif recurs at regular intervals — mark the position of each motif with light pencil lines and a ruler. Or baste a strip of paper along the edge of the fabric, just below the border, marking on it the shapes and colors.

Here are some motifs for a children's party table. They are all made up of simple shapes which you can draw and transfer onto a paper template with dressmaker's carbon paper before cutting into the potato stamp.

Materials for potato printing:
1. A small sharp knife.
2. Very fresh potatoes.
3. Permanent fabric printing colors.
4. Turpentine.
5. Several small pots for mixing paints (egg cups, yoghurt pots, etc.).
6. A glass for the turpentine – to clean the brushes between colors.
7. Fabric scraps for printing tests.
8. Inexpensive paint brushes: one for each color.
9. A fine-tipped pen.
10. White paper. Paper towels.
11. A ruler and compass for marking the position of the motifs. Scissors.
12. A clean working surface.
13. Tracing paper and dressmaker's carbon paper for transferring the motifs.
14. Pins or tacks to secure fabric.
15. Various shapes (pastry cutters, film tins, etc.)

4 Cut the potato straight down the middle, round it off, and leave it to dry on paper towels.

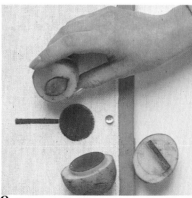

8 Print one shape close to the next one until the motif is complete. Let each layer dry before overprinting.

Potato printing

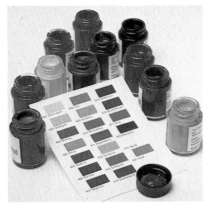

1 Permanent fabric printing colors come in a wide range of shades which will create bright motifs.

2 Assemble all of the working materials. Use large kidney-shaped potatoes for the printing.

3 The motif can be sketched or transferred onto white paper. Draw round it and cut out.

5 Pin the paper design to the flat surface of the potato and cut around it for a cleanly-shaped stamp.

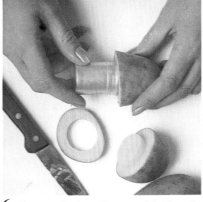

6 For a circle, dig an old film tin into the potato. Cut away the surrounding ring of potato.

7 Spread paint onto the felt; allow it to be absorbed. Press the stamp onto the felt, then onto the fabric.

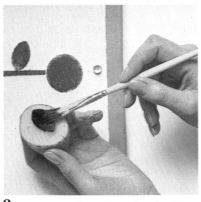

9 You can also print clearly if you paint the color onto the stamp with a paint brush.

10 Press the printed parts on the wrong side with a hot iron. This fixes the color to the fabric.

Hints

Keep a different stamp for each color, to avoid creating muddy-looking mixtures of colors.

Printing errors: slightly irregular motifs can look just as pretty as very regular ones. Obvious mistakes can be painted with white fabric color and reprinted when dry.

Submerge potato stamps in cold water to keep them fresh. They will keep for one to two days in the refrigerator.

Let freshly-cut stamps dry for a while before beginning to print. Dry stamps print more clearly.

Cheap glasses from a department store are gaily painted.

Paint these glasses for your children's birthday parties.

Glassy looks

Painting on glass is an unusual hobby with great potential for budding artists. Begin with our motifs, tracing the outlines from the pattern. As you develop a feel for the materials, try some designs of your own.

The designs are given full size on the pattern.

Materials Required:
Enamel paints for glass painting: brown, red, olive, dark blue, white, black, lilac, and yellow. Fine and medium paintbrushes. Adhesive tape.

Painting the glass
Before painting, make sure the glass is free of grease and dust spots. Cut out the desired motif from the trace pattern, leaving about 1 cm ($\frac{3}{8}$") all around the edges. Stick it under the sheet of glass or inside the glasses with adhesive tape. Stir the paint thoroughly.
Now you can begin painting, following the outlines of the pattern. First fill in the larger areas, smoothly and let them dry well (the surface dries in about 4 hours). This is important as the paint runs easily when wet. Then paint in the details such as the features, the flower centers and the outlines with the fine brush.
When the motifs are complete, leave the object to dry. It will take about 3 days to dry completely.
To make a finished edge around square or rectangular pictures, edge the glass with colored tape, catching in rings for hanging. Alternatively, surround with metal channeling and solder on rings for hanging.

A flower arrangement will fill a corner of your window.

Paint this
quaint couple
for a
cottage setting.

Painting on glass

Special glass paints are used for these charming
motifs which can be applied to tumblers,
plaques, or even windows.

These plain plates have been painted with a black rim, a colored circle in the center, and a bee motif which can be seen actual size, opposite.

Paint a set of mugs and a jug with a cloud motif and a variety of stylized fruit. The fruit motifs are shown actual size overleaf. The paints are just as effective on dark china as on white.

Here is one way to brighten a child's day when a cold or flu means that she can't play.

Funny faces painted onto little pitchers will be sure to make the children laugh. The faces can be given different expressions quite easily by changing the features.

Bon appetit!

Children love to have their own special mugs and plates, and would be delighted with this gaily-painted china. All you need is plain china and Deka hobby paints. Let the children choose a few simple motifs such as flowers and animals or use the ideas given here. You don't have to be a great artist to reproduce bold designs such as the ones illustrated. Overleaf are a few tips for using the paint.

1 On the mug, paint the cloud shape first as a base. You can easily do this freehand as the shape is very simple and can be corrected without difficulty if you do make a mistake.

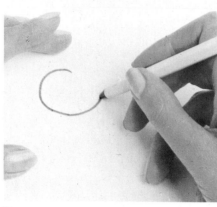

2 If you don't wish to paint the fruit motif freehand, make a stencil to help you. Trace the shape at the bottom of the page onto thin cardboard and cut it out accurately.

3 When the white paint of the cloud is dry, place the stencil over the mug and fill in the apple shape in green paint. Make sure the stencil is positioned correctly and hold it very still.

4 Paint the leaf on the apple with or without a stencil. Leave the paint to dry again. Finally, outline the apple and the leaf with fine brush strokes in black.

Painting on china is easy

Here are a few tips for painting your china.

Deka hobby paints are suitable for glass, plastics, ceramics, pottery, and china as well as other solid materials. Before you begin, make sure that the article to be painted is clean and free of dust and greasy fingerprints. Stir the paint well before applying it.

Use a soft brush to achieve even coverage. The thinner the paint, the quicker it will dry. After about 4 hours, the surface paint will have dried; after about 60 hours, the paint will be completely dry.

It can be hardened further on glass, pottery, and china articles by "baking" them in the oven at least one day after the last application of paint. Place the articles in a cold oven and heat it up to 120°C to 150°C (250°F to 300°F). Turn the oven off after 30–40 minutes, leaving the china to cool. Heating the paint in this way has the advantage of making the colors more scratch-proof and water-resistant. In fact, the paint has excellent durability and washability, but, all the same, it is not advisable to paint areas on which knives or other sharp implements will be used.

Here are the fruit motifs on the jug and the set of mugs shown actual size. Use the same method for painting the orange, lemon, and strawberry as described above for the apple.

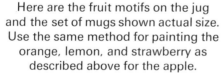

Take an armful

Try out your artistic skills by painting your own wooden bangles in colors to match your clothes. Bold shapes and simple patterns are the most effective.

Materials Required:

Wooden bangles. Poster or enamel paints. Clear varnish.

Plain, untreated wooden bangles should be used. If you have difficulty in obtaining them, large wooden curtain rings are a similar size and make an excellent substitute.

Painting the bangles

Before painting, it may be necessary to sand the bangles with fine sandpaper to smooth the surface. Paint each bangle in its background color first and, when this is completely dry, mark on the design lightly with a sharp pencil.

A regular design such as the multi-colored zigzag pattern must be planned carefully. Measure the circumference of the bangle and divide it into suitable sections so that the zigzag runs regularly around it. Mark upper and lower points with a dot, then join them freehand in the first color, using a fine paintbrush. When dry, add the next colored zigzag and so on. Similarly, for the flower pattern, divide the bangle into regular sections and paint flowers at alternate intervals along each side. Finally, coat with clear varnish.

3

It's a frame-up

7

8

12

13

16

Here are lots of bright ideas for revamping old picture frames or decorating new frames by picking out the colors in favorite pictures or photographs. We have ideas for all shapes and sizes of frame. All you need are enamel paints, brushes, a ruler, a pencil, masking tape, cardboard, and scissors.

1 Outline the inner edge of the frame with a narrow band of blue and a wide band of green. The rest of the frame is painted white with a blue surround.

2 First paint the yellow sides, then the dark green ones. The green stripes at the corners are painted over the yellow. Stick masking tape along the edges for straight lines.

3 Paint as for 1, using pink on the frame to pick out the pink dress in the picture.

4 Paint the whole frame green. Draw lines with a pencil and ruler and fill in the pink stripes.

5 Paint the whole frame green, then draw pencil lines all around it about 0.5 cm ($\frac{1}{4}''$) apart. Fill in the stripes radiating from the center in black.

6 Paint the frame pale blue, then draw in the graduated stripes. Fill in the stripes with dark blue paint. The pale blue paint can be mixed from dark blue and white in equal proportions.

7 First paint the background in yellow, then stick masking tape on the frame in a zigzag pattern and paint over it in green. Remove the tape.

8 An attractive idea for a square frame. Paint the frame yellow. Then draw in diagonal lines with a pencil and ruler, and fill in the stripes in red.

9 Paint the background yellow. For the border, make a diamond-patterned stencil and fill in with red paint.

10 Divide the frame into quarters and, sticking masking tape where the edges meet, paint two quarters light green and two quarters dark green.

11 First paint the central area magenta, then the outer red parts. Stick masking tape at either side for the stripes and fill in with yellow paint.

12 For this unusual frame, first paint the background blue. Then cut a stencil for the star motif and paint on the white stars evenly around the frame.

13 Paint the whole frame green for the background. For stripes, stick on masking tape and fill in with blue.

14 Paint the frame green, then scatter little flowers over it by dotting them on in white and yellow with a fine brush.

15 Another idea for a square frame. Paint the background yellow, then stick two evenly-spaced rows of masking tape around it, stopping short at the outer corners. Fill in the stripes in purple.

16 First paint the frame pale blue. Then, using masking tape to outline the triangular shapes, fill in the medium blue areas next and finally the dark blue areas in the center.

Note: After painting your frame, leave it to dry, then give it a protective coat of varnish. Insert the picture and hang.

Paint a posy

These little painted boxes make excellent presents for birthdays or Christmas, especially if they are filled with mouth-watering sweets.

The small, unpainted wooden boxes are available from craft shops. The floral patterns shown here have been designed to stand out in relief using a mixture of chalk and wood glue which sets hard on drying. Experiment with the consistency of the paste before you begin, mixing it until it is thick, but malleable enough to paint on easily.

The actual size motif for the round box: cut a template out of cardboard or transfer it with carbon paper.

Materials Required: Chalk in powder form. Wood glue. Poster paint: White and desired colors. Wooden boxes. Clear varnish. Paint brushes: fine and thick.

Decorating the boxes

Paint your box with white paint and leave to dry well. Trace the motifs from the actual-size photographs given here, or design some of your own. Transfer the outlines onto the box with carbon paper or cut out cardboard templates. Make a mixture of chalk and wood glue, but check the consistency on a spare piece of wood before applying to the box. It should form a thick paste, which is still malleable enough to be painted on with a brush. Apply this paste onto the parts which are to stand out in relief, *ie*. flowers, leaves, stems, and so on. Build up the paste in layers, depending on how thick the motifs are to be. You can use the handle of the brush to make indentations in the petals and leaves for a more textured effect. Leave the paste to dry well. Paint the larger relief areas first, then paint on the background color. Finally, add finer details such as small leaves. Varnish when dry.

The designs on the oval boxes are shown here actual size.

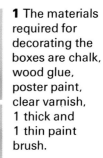

1 The materials required for decorating the boxes are chalk, wood glue, poster paint, clear varnish, 1 thick and 1 thin paint brush.

2 First, paint the box with white paint. Cut a template from cardboard and draw around it onto the well-dried box lid with a sharp pencil. Alternatively, transfer the motif with carbon paper.

3 Make a paste from the chalk and wood glue with a thick, but malleable consistency. Paint on until the motif stands out in relief. Leave to dry. Paint the large relief areas in desired colors.

4 When the paint has dried, fill in the background carefully. Paint in the small details such as stems and dots. Add shading on the flowers.

5 When the box is completely dry, spray or paint it with clear varnish to protect the surface from dust and damage.

1 This tobacco box is simple, but effective. The only decorations are the letters and stripes, two at the lid edge and one around the base. Make or buy a stencil for the letters and work out the spacing carefully.

2 Geometric patterns often look much more complicated than they actually are. Try this one out first on paper. Divide the circle into eight parts. Connect the end of each line to the ends of the other lines. Paint in shades of one color.

3 The design on this box is also basically simple. Divide the circle into four parts, then each part into eight sections. Mark the zigzag line around the edge. Paint alternately light green and dark green with a black background.

4 To make the star motif, divide the circle into eight parts. Divide each line in half, then draw a square so that two corners touch the end and half-line mark and the other two touch the next squares.

Painted wood

Razzle dazzle boxes

These colorful and decorative containers were once plain wooden boxes bought from a crafts shop. Painted and filled with little surprises like sweets or nuts, they make original presents. They are also useful about the house for storing those odds and ends that never seem to find a home, like games pieces, paper clips, pins, rubber bands, etc. Plain wooden boxes come in many shapes and sizes, and can be made from thin wood like the ones shown here, or from sturdier wood with hinged lids.

If you like pop motifs, these boxes are for you. Instructions for transferring the motifs to the boxes are given overleaf. If these designs are not to your taste, look out for other ideas in children's comics, magazines, and on posters if you are not confident enough to draw your own.

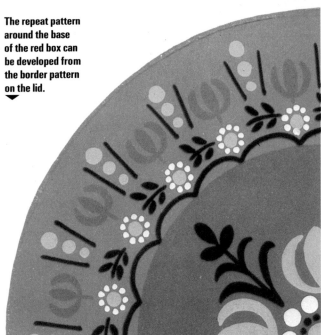

Three folk designs to trace

Before transferring the design, paint the box in the base color with acrylic or poster paint. Light colors which do not cover well should have two coats.

The designs for the boxes in the top photograph on the previous page are given here. They can be transferred onto the box tops as follows: Place tracing paper over the designs and trace them in pencil very carefully.

To position the pattern correctly, divide the box top into halves or quarters, marking it lightly with a soft pencil. Then transfer the design onto the box. Transfer the design with carbon paper, going over the lines of the design with a pencil. Half the floral pattern is given; to transfer the other half, turn the tracing paper over. A quarter of

the other two designs is given, so transfer this quarter four times, reversing the tracing paper as required.

If possible, go over the lines of the pattern with a felt-tip pen in the relevant colors of the sections. In this way, the boundaries will be neater than those made with a soft paint brush.

Now paint the design with the acrylic or poster

paint, using a soft brush. Finally, varnish the box to give it a glossy appearance and to make it easier to dust.

The geometric patterns shown at the beginning of the chapter can be drawn straight onto the box top after practising on a piece of paper. Use a soft pencil which will not scratch the base paint and can be rubbed out if you make a mistake.

Long skirts with flowers
Fiesta fashions

If you like unusual clothes with great impact, then why not paint flowers on a ruffled peasant skirt and shawl with fabric paints. The motifs are given as an actual-size pattern.

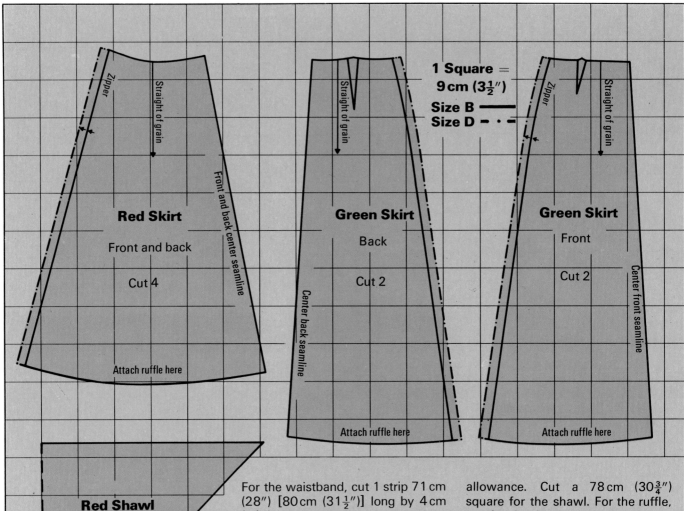

Red Skirt

Front and back

Cut 4

Attach ruffle here

Zipper

Straight of grain

Front and back center seamline

Green Skirt

Back

Cut 2

Center back seamline

Straight of grain

Attach ruffle here

1 Square = 9 cm (3½")

Size B ——

Size D —·—·—

Green Skirt

Front

Cut 2

Zipper

Straight of grain

Center front seamline

Attach ruffle here

Red Shawl

Cut 1

Half-pattern line

Straight of grain

To enlarge the pattern, draw a grid of 9 cm (3½") squares on tissue or tracing paper and transfer pattern outlines to new grid.

Sizes: B for 63.5 cm or 25" waist, 90 cm or 35½" hip and D for 72.5 cm or 28½" waist, 98 cm or 38½" hip. Measurements for larger size are in square brackets.

RED SKIRT

Materials Required: Cotton: 6 m (6½ yds) [6.1 m (6⅔ yds)], 90 cm (36") wide. Waistband interfacing: 2 cm (¾") wide to fit waist. Hooks and eyes. Zipper. Thread.

Cutting out: Add a 2 cm (¾") seam allowance to all pieces. For ruffle, cut 5 straight strips from selvage to selvage, each 32 cm (12⅝") wide.

For the waistband, cut 1 strip 71 cm (28") [80 cm (31½")] long by 4 cm (1½"), plus seam allowance.

Sewing: Stitch the ruffle strips in 1 long strip, ready for painting, but do not make a circle. Transfer motifs with dressmaker's carbon. Paint 8 motifs along the ruffle and a stripe at the hem fold line. Join the skirt pieces at the center front and side seams and paint a stripe along the lower edge. Paint a stripe around the shawl edges and a motif at the center back. Let dry. Then join the center back skirt seam. Join the ruffle to form a circle. Turn up the hem, gather the ruffle and stitch to the skirt. Sew in the zipper and gather the skirt to fit the waist measurement. Make a waistband with a 3 cm (1¼") overlap. Sew on hooks and eyes. Shawl: turn under the raw edges twice and stitch.

GREEN SKIRT

Materials Required: Cotton: 3.70 m (4 yds) [3.80 (4⅛ yds)], 90 cm (36") wide. Waistband interfacing: 3 cm (1¼") wide to fit waist. Hooks and eyes. Zipper. Thread.

Cutting out: Add a 2 cm (¾") seam allowance. Cut a 78 cm (30¾") square for the shawl. For the ruffle, cut 4 strips from selvage to selvage, each 19 cm (7½") wide. For the waistband, cut a strip 71 cm (28") [80 cm (31½")] long and 6 cm (2½") wide, plus seam allowances.

Sewing: Stitch the darts in the skirt back and front pieces. Join the center seams and one side seam. Transfer motifs with dressmaker's carbon. Paint 2 double rows of stripes 1 cm (⅜") and 20 cm (8") from the lower edge. Paint 3 motifs each on the front and back between these stripes. On the shawl, paint 2 stripes all around edges and a motif in one corner. Let dry. Join the other side seam of the skirt. Join the ruffle strips into a circle. On one long side, turn under a 3 cm (1¼") wide hem; on the other side, finish raw edge with zigzag stitch, then make a small head by turning under a 1.5 cm (⅝") seam allowance. Gather ruffle. Stitch to skirt. Make waistband with a 3 cm (1¼") overlap and stitch to the skirt. Sew on hooks and eyes. To make the shawl, fold in half, turn in the raw edges, and top-stitch all around.

Painting on cotton fabric

The flowers on the peasant skirts are painted onto the cotton with fabric paints. For the red and white flowers, you need carmine, white, pale green, dark green, and yellow. For the blue and red flowers, you need blue, carmine, green, white, and black. Fabric colors can normally be fixed by ironing on the reverse side of the fabric.

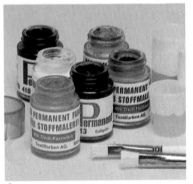

1 <u>Materials Required</u>: permanent fabric paints, 2 bristle paint brushes, paper cups for mixing, masking tape.

2 Stick tape along the fabric edges to make the stripes straight. Paint slightly over the tape, then peel it off.

3 Red/white flowers: Trace and transfer the motifs. Paint in white and pale green, covering the transfer lines neatly.

4 For the shading, dip the brush into the paint once, draw a curve, and smooth the paint outwards from it gradually.

5 For the shading on the leaves, lightly apply a little dark green. Leave to dry well and fix by ironing on the wrong side.

6 Blue/red flowers: Trace and transfer the motifs. Paint the flowers in basic colors of red and blue, the leaves in green.

7 Now add the shading to the petals and leaves. Mix red, blue, and green with a little black to produce darker areas.

8 Finally, paint in the highlights by mixing white with the other colors. Leave to dry and fix by ironing on the wrong side.

Flowers for
Red Skirt

72

Flower painting on fabric

Use special fabric paints to decorate the edge of a long skirt with colorful blooms. Paint a shawl, too, to complete the outfit.

Flowers for
Green Skirt

1

2

3

Wax works

You can make wonderful pictures on clothes and articles for the house with the ancient craft of batik. The fabric we have used is pure cotton, which has been boiled first to remove the sizing or dressing. Cut out the part to be decorated with generous allowances, then trace the motifs from the pattern and work as shown overleaf. At each dyeing stage, dye the rest of the fabric pieces, too, so that they come out the same shade. The following quantities of dye are adequate for 2 liters ($3\frac{1}{2}$ pints) of water. For larger pieces of fabric, increase the quantities in the same ratio.

Brown: First dyeing, $\frac{1}{2}$ teaspoon. Second dyeing, 15 gm ($\frac{1}{2}$ oz).

Green: First dyeing, $\frac{1}{2}$ teaspoon. Second dyeing, 15 gm ($\frac{1}{2}$ oz).

Blue: First dyeing, 2 teaspoons of light blue. 2nd dyeing, 15 gm ($\frac{1}{2}$ oz) of dark blue.

Making the articles

1 Cushions: Each measures 40 cm ($15\frac{3}{4}$") square. Cut out the fabric 40 cm x 80 cm ($15\frac{3}{4}$" x $31\frac{1}{2}$"), plus seam allowance. Stitch and turn; insert a zipper into the fourth side.

2 Head scarves: Each is a right-angled triangle with 75 cm, 75 cm, and 106 cm ($29\frac{1}{2}$", $29\frac{1}{2}$", and $41\frac{3}{4}$") sides or 60 cm, 60 cm, and 85 cm ($23\frac{5}{8}$", $23\frac{5}{8}$", and $33\frac{1}{2}$") sides. Add 1 cm ($\frac{3}{8}$") all around for the hem. Turn the edges in twice and stitch.

3 Dress: Choose a dressmaking pattern in a simple style with a large pocket. Cut out all pieces to be decorated on the straight of grain.

4 Wall hanging: Cut a piece of fabric 76 cm x 66 cm (30" x 26"), adding 2 cm ($\frac{3}{4}$") at the sides and 4 cm ($1\frac{1}{2}$") at top and bottom. Turn in the sides twice and stitch. Make a casing at top and bottom 3 cm ($1\frac{1}{4}$") wide. Insert dowelling and nail wooden balls to the ends.

5 Woman's dress: Choose a dressmaking pattern in a simple style with a plain bodice or large pocket. Cut out all pieces to be decorated on the straight of grain.

Batik: making pictures with wax and dyes

In batik, all areas not to be colored are waxed so that the dye cannot penetrate the fabric. Pretty effects can be obtained with one dye only or with several different colors.

1 Materials required for your batik work: Batik dyes. Batik wax. One wide and one narrow brush. One wooden frame and thumb tacks. White candle ends. A saucepan and a tin can. A plastic bowl or bucket for dyeing. Vinegar. You will also need an iron and old newspapers for removing the wax, plus turpentine for a final cleaning. The most suitable fabric is white or off-white cotton.

4 For the first dyeing, the lightest color is always used. Mix the quantity of dye stated in the bowl with 1 tablespoon of salt to every 2 liters ($3\frac{1}{2}$ pts) of boiling water. Leave the water to cool down to a maximum of 35°C (95°F) otherwise it will melt the wax. If possible, test the color first on a piece of the same fabric. Leave the fabric in the bowl for at least 5 minutes, stirring it constantly. Leave to dry in a cool place. Next, paint all the areas that are to remain the pale color with wax. Place the fabric once more into a dye bath with the next darkest color or shade, and so on, with the colors becoming progressively darker. After the last dye bath, rinse out the fabric, adding a spoonful of vinegar to the water. Press out the fabric carefully, instead of wringing it out, as the wax will be hard.

2 Wash the fabric to eliminate any sizing or dressing and to shrink it. Trace the motifs onto the fabric with pencil or tailor's chalk (not carbon paper). Stretch fabric over wooden frame.

3 Melt the candle ends in the can placed in a saucepan of water, then add batik wax. When this has melted, paint all areas and lines that are to remain white with liquid wax.

5 Finally, the wax is ironed out through several layers of newspaper. Remove any remaining wax with turpentine.

A detail of the wall hanging shows how the motifs are built up. Some areas remain white, others are pale green, and the rest are dark green.

Batik designs

Here are some simple motifs for batik beginners. Try them on cushions, on a wall hanging, or on a pretty pinafore dress.

Collect the materials – leaves and lichen – on walks in the country or by the sea.

The natural dye is produced by boiling the gathered materials for an hour or two in water. By adding various chemicals, the color shades can be altered. ▼

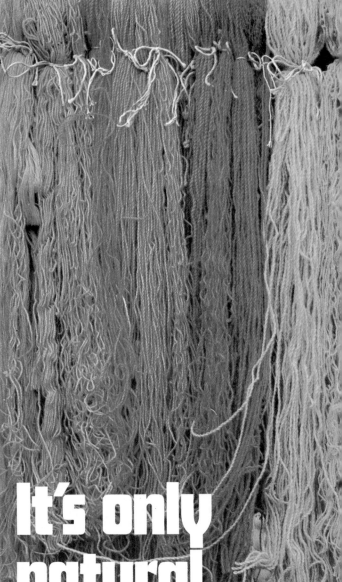

It's only natural

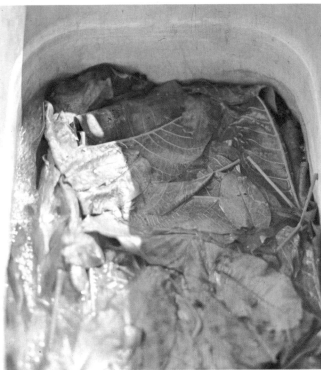

If you have ever experienced the frustration of a fruitless search for a subtle shade of wool for your knitting or weaving, you may find that the answer is to dye your own yarn. Nature provides a wealth of materials – leaves, flowers, roots, lichens, and berries – which produce colors with a beautiful, rich lustre.

Materials and Equipment: You may be lucky enough to have a special room that can be set aside for dyeing equipment, or, if you live in the country, you can dye on an open fire outside, but otherwise an ordinary kitchen stove will do. Other equipment includes large aluminium, stainless steel, or enamel

vessels which can hold about 15 liters (26½ pints) to dye 250gm (9oz) of wool, or 5 liters (11 pints) to dye 100gm (4oz) of wool. Smooth wooden sticks for stirring. Pair of scales. Kitchen thermometer. Rubber gloves. Wool for dyeing should be white without any added synthetic fibers. Test-dye a small sample first, as different wools accept colors in different intensities.

The dye plants for which we have given recipes here are birch and walnut leaves and lichen which produce dyes in the yellow, green, and brown color ranges. Gather the leaves in early summer and the lichen in winter or after long periods of rain when they can be

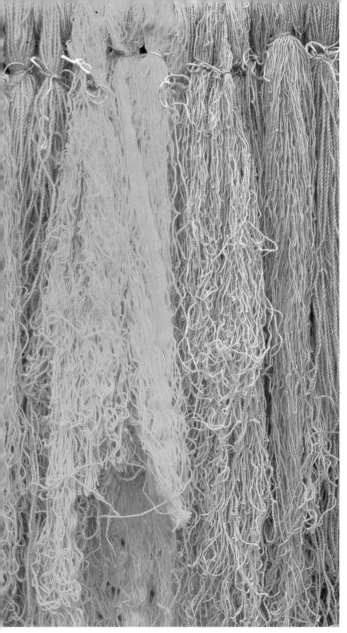

Before the first dipping, the wool is wound into hanks and tied with thread securely, but not too tightly, so that the mordant and dye can penetrate well into the woollen fibers.

Mordanting involves dissolving metal salts (which enable the fiber to absorb the dye) in hot water. Before the mordanting process, the wool is warmed up in clear water.

The mordanting takes about one hour. During this time, the wool is rotated on sticks so that the woollen fibers are evenly dipped and penetrated.

scraped off more easily. Dry the plants and use them at any time of the year. They can be used fresh too, but you will have to double the amount.

Mordanting and Dyeing

Two processes are normally required: the preparation (called the mordanting) and the dyeing itself. The mordants are chemicals which are absorbed by the fibers and fix the dye.

Mordanting: Make sure the wool is clean before you begin. Wind it into hanks of about 100 gm (4 oz) in weight and 130 cm (50") in circumference. Then tie linen thread loosely around the hank in 4 places, dip into warm water 40°C (104°F) for 5 minutes, and

wring out. This warms the wool before it is placed in the mordanting or dyeing bath, saving it from sudden alterations in temperature to which it is sensitive.

Dissolve the chemicals given in the recipe in warm water. Put the hank into the mordanting bath and moisten it evenly. This is done by looping the wool around the two smooth wooden sticks. With one stick in each hand, dip the wool about half way into the bath and rotate so that a new section continually enters the bath and is rotated upward. Then dip the whole hank into the bath. Heat slowly to simmering point, then simmer gently for about 1 hour. From the hot steeping, the wool can either be put straight into the hot dye [difference in temperature should be no more than 30°C (86°F)], or left to cool in the solution until the dye bath is ready. You can also steep and dry the wool in advance.

Dyeing: When dyeing, the first quarter of an hour is crucial for even coloring. To avoid patchiness, rotate the hank continually but gently around two sticks as described above. Then dip the wool under completely and stir only occasionally. If other chemicals have to be added according to the recipe, remove the wool first together with some of the liquid. Dissolve the chemicals and then put the wool back into the dye bath. After dyeing, wash the wool in luke-warm water 40°C (104°F) to remove excess dye. Then rinse it very throroughly in cold water until no more color comes away. Hang up the skeins of wool on smooth sticks to dry, not too close together. Weight them slightly to stretch the fibers. Dry in the shade or a well-aired position indoors.

Washing the wool: The color-fastness of wool varies after dyeing, so never use strong detergents for washing; rinse in a light solution of soap flakes at 50°–70°C (122°–158°F) for 10 minutes.

Dye recipes
Quantities are given for dyeing 100gm (4oz) and 250gm (9oz) of yarn. Figures in square brackets refer to 250gm (9oz). Use dried leaves, or double quantities for fresh leaves.

Yellow
Mordanting: 20gm ($\frac{3}{4}$oz) [50gm (2oz)] alum; 5l (11pts) [12.5l (27$\frac{1}{4}$pts)] water.
Dyeing: 100gm (4oz) [250gm (9oz)] birch leaves; 5l (11pts) [12.5l (27$\frac{1}{4}$pts)] water.
Simmer the yarn in alum solution for 1 hour at 90°C (194°F) and leave to cool in it. Boil the birch leaves for 1 hour in given quantity of water and strain. Place yarn in luke-warm water, wring out, and dip in dye for 1 hour at 90°C (194°F). Then rinse well in luke-warm water 40°C (104°F). The dyed yarn will be reddish-yellow if it is left unwashed after dyeing and then put into a potash solution of 1gm to 1 liter water (0.03oz to 2$\frac{1}{4}$pints water). Rinse and dry.

Grey-green
Mordant with alum and then dye as for yellow. After an hour, take the yarn out of the dye bath and add iron vitriol (also called ferrous sulphate or copperas) to solution, adding 10 gm ($\frac{3}{8}$oz) for 250gm (9oz) yarn; add 5gm ($\frac{1}{8}$oz) for 100gm (4oz) yarn. Then dip the yarn again for 15 minutes at 90°C (194°F), rotating through the bath with sticks. Finally, rinse well in vinegar water.

Vinegar water: Use 50ml (1$\frac{3}{4}$fluid oz) vinegar to 1l (2$\frac{1}{4}$pts) water.

Olive green
Mordant and dye as for grey-green. In place of iron vitriol, add the same quantity of copper vitriol (copper sulphate) and again wash and rinse in vinegar water.

Brown (with walnut leaves)
Mordanting: 15gm ($\frac{1}{2}$oz) [35gm (1$\frac{1}{4}$oz)] alum; 5l (11pts) [12.5l (27$\frac{1}{4}$pts)] water.
Dyeing: 0.5kg (1lbs) [1kg (2$\frac{1}{4}$lbs)] walnut leaves; 5l (11pts) [12.5l (27$\frac{1}{4}$pts)] water.
Steep yarn in alum solution for 1 hour at 90°C (194°F). Boil the walnut leaves for 1–2 hours in water and strain. Dip the steeped yarn in the dye for 1 hour then rinse. The fluid can be reused for a lighter color.

Brown (with lichen)
Lichen can be found on stones and rocks, especially near the sea or on moorland or mountains.
Mordanting: 20gm ($\frac{3}{4}$oz) [50gm (2oz)] alum; 10gm ($\frac{3}{8}$oz) [25gm (1oz)] cream of tartar; 5l (11pts) [12.5l (27$\frac{1}{4}$pts)] water.
Dyeing: 400gm (14oz) [1kg (2$\frac{1}{4}$lbs)] lichen; 5gm ($\frac{1}{8}$oz) [10gm ($\frac{3}{8}$oz)] iron vitriol.
Steep the yarn in a solution of alum and cream of tartar for 1 hour at 90°C (194°F). Having soaked the lichen on the previous day, boil it for 1–2 hours in the required amount of water and strain. Dip the damp, wrung-out yarn in the dye for 2 hours at 90°C (194°F), moving it around carefully. Take yarn out of bath, add iron vitriol and stir well. When dissolved, treat yarn in dye bath again for 15 minutes at 90°C (194°F) and rinse in vinegar water. The color will be dark brown. If copper vitriol is used in place of iron vitriol, a red-brown shade results.

When the leaves have been simmered for long enough, the dye mixture is strained. The wool is left in the hot dye bath for at least an hour and stirred to absorb color evenly.

Finally, the dyed wool is washed in luke-warm water, then rinsed in cold water and hung up in a well-ventilated place to dry.

On the cards

Try your hand at card or tablet weaving and make a long, gaily-colored belt. We show you how overleaf.

FOR BOTH BELTS

You will need remnants of cotton or wool yarns of equal thickness. A fine cotton will work as well as a medium-thick wool. However, the thinner the strands, the narrower the belt will be.

GREEN BELT

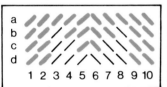

Yarn: 28 strands green, 12 strands white, yarn for weft.
Making the belt: See the How-to.

PINK BELT

Yarn: 16 strands each pink and white, 8 strands aubergine, yarn for weft.
Making the belt: Thread the cards and make them into a block, following the diagonal lines on the diagram. Weave as for the Green Belt (instructions are given in How-to), but make alternately 12 quarter turns upward and downward. When completed, knot the ends of the warp strands as for the Green Belt.

Card or tablet weaving

Tablet or card weaving produces long bands with ethnic-looking patterns which make wonderful belts. Using the green-and-white belt (left) as an example, we explain the method in step-by-step photographs.

You can buy the square cards or make them yourself from firm cardboard by cutting 6 cm x 6 cm (2¼″ x 2¼″) squares, smoothing the edges, and rounding off the corners with sandpaper. Then drill a hole 0.5 cm (¼″) in diameter in each corner, 0.5 cm (¼″) from the edge (you may be able to use a hole punch). In order to work the pattern, the cards are numbered and lettered. Mark the holes **a, b, c, d** on one side, then on the other side mark the same holes with the

identical letters (see diagram). Each card is also numbered; for the green belt, you will require 10 cards. To simplify the weaving process, color the upper edge of the cards (between holes **a** and **b**). We have marked ours in white.

The pattern diagram for the green belt is shown here; the letters at the side indicate the holes, the numbers below indicate the cards. The color shows the color of the strand to be threaded through the relevant holes and the direction of the lines shows how the cards must be placed after the thread is pulled through. See photographs 1–3.

Cutting the threads: For each warp strand, allow the length of the belt, plus 50 cm (19½″). Cut as many strands of each color as is shown in the diagram. For this belt, cut 28 green and 12 white. For the weft strand, use the same color as for the warp strands of the two outside cards. (1 and 10). The length is optional, but the longer the weft strand, the less often you will have to add in a new one.

Threading the cards: The direction of the lines in the diagram are significant – when the line runs from the bottom left to top right, then hole **a** must be at the top right. When the line runs from bottom right to top left, the card must be placed so that hole **a** is at the top left.

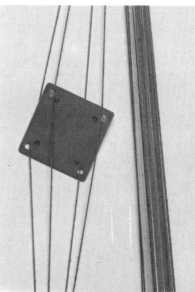

1 Here you can see how the first tablet is threaded and placed so that hole **a** points upward. Thread the first 5 cards in this way and position them one on top of the other with the same letters placed together.

2 This photograph shows how card No. 10 is threaded. As you will notice, the letters are in exactly the reverse order. Thread cards 9–6 in this way, placing the same letters together. Hole **a** points upward here, too. After you have threaded each card, always

84

2

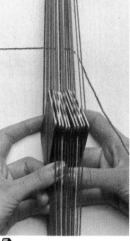

knot together the 4 strands at the upper end. Now place the 2 sets of cards together by putting the left-hand set against the right-hand one so that you have a block in which all **a, b, c,** and **d** holes lie over one another. The marked white edges should lie parallel to the warp threads.

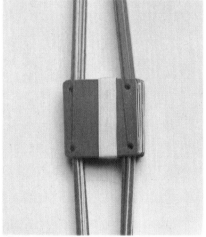

3 Tie this block together securely with, for example, a rubber band and safety pin. Hold the knotted strand ends together, insert string through the loops and fasten the bundle onto a stable object such as a table. Draw up the other ends until equally taut and fasten, too, by wrapping around a board and sitting on it when weaving. The tauter you manage to stretch the threads and the better you secure them, the easier it is to turn the cards.

4 Undo the rubber band when weaving. Thread the first weft strand through about 20 cm (8″) from the upper end. Hold the cards with both hands and turn them upward a quarter turn.

5 Now holes **b** and **c** lie at the upper edge and the white marked edges **a–b** lie in between the warp strands. The warp strands which come through holes **a** and **d** are on the underside of the work, while those through holes **b** and **c** are on the upper side. Take the weft strand through.

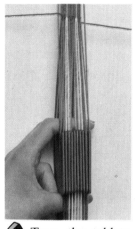

6 Turn the tablets upward again and take the weft strand through. Push it up.

7 After 4 turns, the cards are back at the starting position and one repeat pattern is completed.

When the weft thread comes to an end, join in a new one by weaving the two together for about 4 rows. Cut off the loose ends later.

8 After a certain number of turns, the same process is repeated in the other direction. In this case, turn the cards upward 13 times, downward 13 times and so on.

9 After each series of forward and backward turns, there is a break and the pattern is reversed. When the belt is long enough, undo both ends, stitch down the beginning and end of the weft strands and knot the strand threads securely, leaving tassels hanging at ends.

Woven in strips and sewn together

Fabrication

Be ingenious with your oddments of fabric and weave yourself a handsome rag rug. Tough and practical, it fits in beautifully with country-style surroundings.

Size: About 170 x 95 cm (67" x 37½").

Materials Required: Fabric: Approximately 1½ kg (3¼ lbs) of cotton remnants. 2 spools of fine, strong warp thread. Simple weaving loom.

Making the rug

The rug illustrated is made up of squares woven in strips which are then sewn together edge to edge. Each square measures about 19 cm x 19 cm (7½" x 7½"). After the first and before the last row of squares, there are 4 stripes 4.5 cm (2") wide. These are made by weaving the same stripe sequence in each of the 5 strips. This gives the illusion of continuous crosswise stripes when sewn together.

Before beginning to work, plan the color sequence and make sure you have enough fabric to repeat the squares if necessary, especially on the narrow stripes.

Prepare and weave the strips as shown overleaf. Begin and end each weft strip with a double row as shown. Weave all other rows over and under alternate threads in plain weave.

When each complete strip is removed from the loom, knot together every 4 warp threads at the beginning and end. Cut them to 4 cm (1⅝") and leave as a fringe. The rug can, of course, be made larger or smaller as required. The pattern, too, can be varied according to the fabrics you have at hand and as your imagination suggests. For example, you could work stripes in between each row of squares, or make a whole rug in stripes of varying colors and widths. If a bright color scheme does not appeal to you, try making the rug in soft, neutral colors such as cream, beige and brown, or grey and off-white.

Delve into your scrap bag for some good-sized remnants of cotton fabric. Cut them into strips and weave a hard-wearing rug – the brighter the better.

Weaving a rag rug on a loom

To weave a rag rug, you will need a simple loom. These are available in different widths in hand-craft shops and have instructions for setting them up provided by the manufacturer. Use a fine, strong warp thread for the rug.

Draw the warp threads through the reed, doubling the outside ones. Fasten them to the warp beam at one end of the loom and wind them up evenly. It is very important that all the threads are equally taut. The other thread ends are fastened to the cloth beam.

The length of the warp threads is estimated in the following way: Required length of rug + 10% + 40 cm (15¾″).

If a warp thread becomes loose during weaving, a quick way to tighten it up is to place a small piece of paper underneath it on the warp beam.

3 To begin, weave shuttle through, leaving a short end. Take the shuttle around the double warp thread at the side and weave it back between the same warp threads.

1 Before beginning to weave, cut each remnant of cotton fabric round and round in a spiral to form a continuous strip about 2 cm (¾″) wide. Cut a curve at each corner rather than a sharp angle.

4 Weave the weft strip through fairly loosely to prevent the width being pulled in as you work from side to side. The weft is pushed together with a wide-toothed comb or heddle to make it firm.

2 Then cut the corners slightly flatter with the scissors. This strip of fabric is wound around the shuttle to form the weft thread.

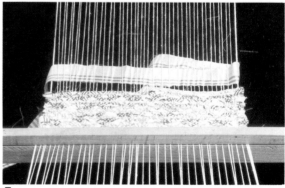

5 To change the weft strip, finish the end of the strip as in photograph 3, push together the weft, and begin the new weft strip in the same way.

Basic techniques of weaving

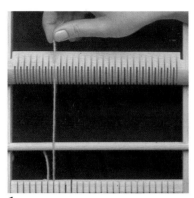

1 Fasten the warp thread onto bottom beam and take it across the heddle to the other side.

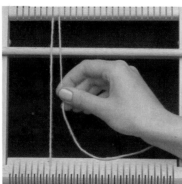
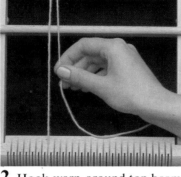

2 Hook warp around top beam groove. Repeat. Each beam and heddle groove holds 1 thread.

There are several different kinds of simple looms available. The photographs on the left show you how to set up and work with one of these looms. Although the appearance of the various parts may vary slightly from loom to loom, the method is basically the same. For the sake of clarity, the warp threads are shown in two colors.

A simple loom has a beam at either end, which may be movable, and a heddle in between, which raises or lowers alternate warp threads in each row to form a space called a shed. The yarn for the weft threads is wound around a shuttle, which is passed through the shed.

When the shuttle is passed through the shed, let the weft lie loosely across the warp, close the shed, and push the weft firmly into place with a beater. To estimate the length of the warp threads, add 10% to the length of the article and about 30 cm ($11\frac{3}{4}''$) for each end of the thread.

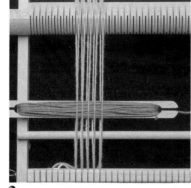

3 For a plain weave, move the heddle to raise the warp threads. Pass the shuttle through.

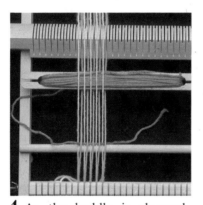

4 As the heddle is changed, alternate warp threads are raised. Pass the shuttle through.

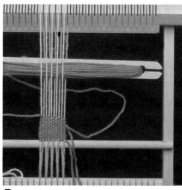

5 To change color for the stripes on belts 4 and 6: Pass the new color on the right under all the warp threads and weave it through from the left.

6 To work the pattern in belts 1 and 2: Pass both shuttles through the shed, weaving them over and under the number of lowered warp threads given.

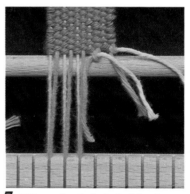

7 When the belt is finished, cut off each pair of warp threads and knot them together. Weave these ends into the work on the wrong side so they do not show.

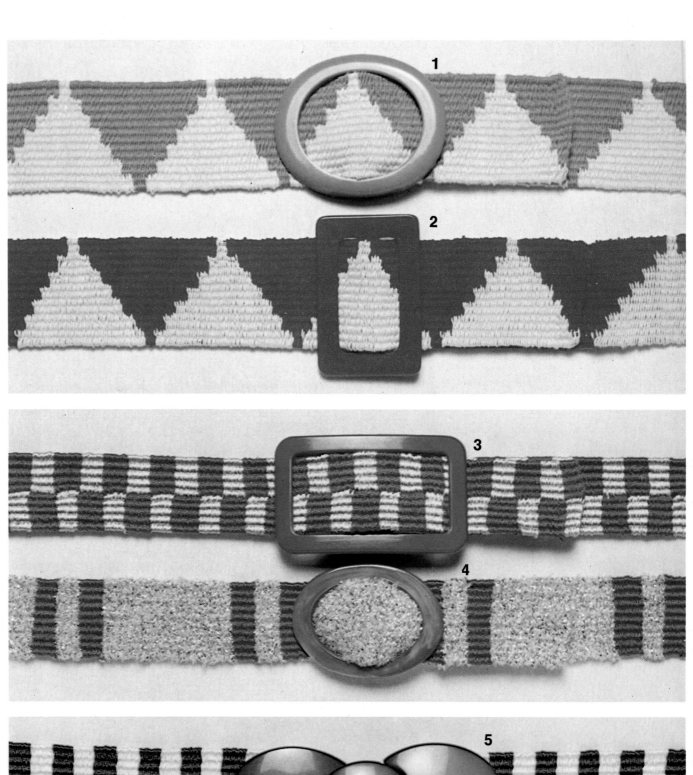

Weaving for beginners

Weave a belt for every dress

Have you ever woven a belt? It's quite easy with a simple loom. Try one with colors and a design to match a dress and finish it with a smart buckle. A petersham or grosgrain ribbon backing will add extra firmness. The number of repeat patterns required will vary according to your waist measurement.

BELTS 1 AND 2

Materials Required: Fine cotton yarn in red or green and beige.

Stretch 14 warp threads onto loom. Weave 10 rows plain weave in green or red.

Row 11: With the beige yarn, work over 1 lowered warp thread and under the remaining 6. In the same shed, pass the green (red) yarn under 1 lowered warp thread and over 6. (For an illustration of this method, see photograph 6 on the basic how-to.)

Row 12: With green (red), work over 6 and under 1 thread. In the same shed pass the beige under 6 and over 1 thread.

Repeat the last 2 rows four more times.

Row 21: With beige, work over 2 and under 5 threads. In the same shed, pass green (red) under 2 and over 5 threads.

Row 22: With green (red), work over 5 and under 2 threads. In the same shed, pass beige under 5 and over 2 threads.

Repeat the last 2 rows four more times.

After every 10 rows, always progress 1 warp thread further in beige, until all the warp threads have been woven with beige. Then repeat the pattern in reverse until all the warp threads have been woven with green (red).

BELTS 3 AND 5

Materials Required: Synthetic yarn in blue and silver, or green and white. Any thin strong yarn for the warp threads.

Stretch 10 warp threads onto the loom. Begin at the right-hand side.

Row 1: With silver (white), work over 2 lowered warp threads and under 3. In the same shed, pass blue (green) under 2 threads and over 3.

Row 2: Work blue (green) over 2 lowered threads and under 3, then pass silver (white) under 2 threads and over 3. Repeat these 2 rows, alternating the two colors every 1 cm ($\frac{3}{8}$").

BELTS 4 AND 6

Materials Required: Synthetic yarn in blue or green. Lurex yarn in silver or red. Any thin strong yarn for the warp threads.

Stretch 10 warp threads onto the loom. Work plain weave for 5 cm (2") in silver or red. Then weave 1 cm ($\frac{3}{8}$") stripes in blue (green), silver (red), and blue (green). Repeat sequence for desired length.

Materials Required:

Carpet tape or webbing: 49.5 m (54 yds), about 8 cm (3″) wide. 2 strong wooden rods: each 95 cm (37½″) long, 2.6 cm (1″) wide, and 3.6 cm (1½″) thick. Rope: 2 pieces each 6 mm (¼″) thick, 6 m (6⅝ yds) long, plus extra for hanging. 2 strong rings 8 cm (3″) in diameter. 2 snap hooks about 10 cm (4″) long. Linen carpet thread. Leather needle (triangular tip). Buttonhole thread.

Making the hammock

Saw the rods into curved shape as shown in the diagram below. Drill six 8 mm (5/16″) holes.
Cut 22 crosswise bands each 114 cm (45″) long and 10 lengthwise bands each 2.36 m (93″) long. On each band, turn one end upward and one end downward 12 cm (4½″) and work zigzag stitch with buttonhole thread. Now place the crosswise bands side by side, with the cut edges facing alternately up or down. At one long side, draw one lengthwise band through every 2nd loop of the crosswise bands,

drawing through those where the cut edges are facing upward. The loose bands between are then fastened along the edge with overcasting. The other long side is woven in the same manner. Then weave the inner rows; the lengthwise bands will cover the raw edges on the crosswise bands. Stitch all around the outer edges through all layers with carpet thread. Now insert the rods. Thread the rope for hanging as shown in the diagram, knotting the ends with a square knot. Fasten snap hooks to rings; draw rope through hook. Fix to tree.

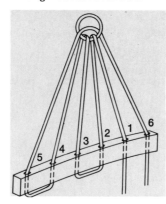

Draw the rope through the holes in the rod as shown here and knot the ends as shown on the right.

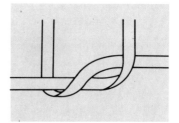

Here we show you how to make a square knot. Cross the strands over each other as shown above.

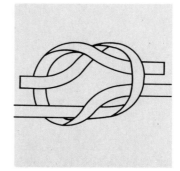

For the second stage of the knot, cross the ends of rope around one another the other way around.

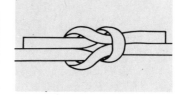

Hold the ends of rope firmly and at the same time pull the knot together tightly to secure.

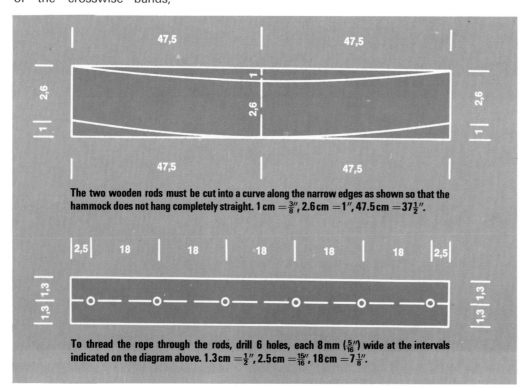

The two wooden rods must be cut into a curve along the narrow edges as shown so that the hammock does not hang completely straight. 1 cm = 3/8″, 2.6 cm = 1″, 47.5 cm = 37½″.

To thread the rope through the rods, drill 6 holes, each 8 mm (5/16″) wide at the intervals indicated on the diagram above. 1.3 cm = ½″, 2.5 cm = 15/16″, 18 cm = 7⅛″.

92

Swing low

Wouldn't you love to while away those lazy summer afternoons swinging gently in a hammock? This one, made of wide carpet webbing, is strong and temptingly comfortable.

Mitering a corner

Using our place mat as an example, we show you here how to miter a corner on a double hem.

1 First, mark the two hem fold lines with basting along the fabric grain. The inner basting line is the outer edge of the mat and lies 3 cm ($1\frac{1}{4}''$) from the outer drawn-through thread. The outer basting line lies 3 cm ($1\frac{1}{4}''$) further out, and 2 cm ($\frac{3}{4}''$) from the outside raw edge. Press along the basting.

2 Now mark the innermost corner formed by the basting threads with a pin and turn the fabric back at an exact diagonal through this corner point. Press down along the fold line.

3 Cut away the corner about 1 cm ($\frac{3}{8}''$) in from the folded edge.

4 Turn in the hem twice and sew down close to the outer drawn-through thread. Slip-stitch the diagonal seam together at the corner, catching in only one thread of the hem at a time.

Setting the mood

For meals in the garden or on the patio, these place mats will fit the bill perfectly. The decorative border is quickly built up by drawing through lengths of pearl cotton in contrasting colors.

Size: 40 cm x 52 cm ($15\frac{3}{4}''$ x $20\frac{1}{2}''$).

Materials Required:
Rectangles of burlap or hessian measuring 54 cm x 66 cm ($21\frac{1}{4}''$ x 26") in red, orange, blue and green. Pearl cotton No. 5: 3 skeins each in red, orange, blue, and green. Sewing thread.

Making the mats
Draw out the threads around the edge of each rectangle for about 1 cm ($\frac{3}{8}''$). Cut pearl cotton into lengths double that of the edges, ie. 132 cm (52") and 108 cm ($42\frac{1}{2}''$). Measure in 9 cm ($3\frac{5}{8}''$) from last thread at outer edge on one side and pull out left-hand end of 1 thread slightly until you can see where right-hand end comes out. Fold a length of pearl cotton in half. Divide

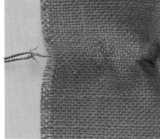

Knot one of the threads around the doubled pearl cotton and pull through the weave of the fabric.

left-hand end of woven thread and knot around the center of the doubled pearl cotton. Press knot flat with your fingers to enable it to slip through fabric more easily. Pull right-hand end of woven thread until it comes right out, drawing pearl cotton with it to replace it. Continue weaving pearl cotton threads from outside toward center of mat as follows: Weave 2 adjacent threads, skip 2 fabric threads, weave 1, skip 2 fabric threads, weave 2, skip 2 fabric threads, weave 1, skip 1 fabric thread, weave 2, skip 3 fabric threads, weave 1. On each place mat, draw through the colors of the other 3 mats in any attractive color sequence. Repeat the same color and weaving sequence on the other 3 sides. Press the mats so that the pearl cotton threads do not pucker the fabric. Then trim off the fabric to 8 cm ($3\frac{1}{4}''$) from the outer pearl cotton threads. Hem the mats, mitering the corners as shown in the How-to photographs opposite.

Let it shine

Cane weaving is not just for baskets — the same method can produce these unusual lampshades which will complement an outdoor setting or an informal family room.

Cane is available in many craft shops and comes in various thicknesses. Two thicknesses of cane are used here — a fairly strong one for the upright stakes or ribs and one 2 to 3 sizes thinner for weaving.

The number of stakes required depends on the size of the object being made. Thick stakes are strong enough to be distributed singly, while thinner ones are used in pairs. To make the cane pliable, soak it in hot water for about 30 minutes before use. If it dries while being woven, resoak it until easy to handle again. For the lampshades, you will also need a large bottle which will produce a neck of the right width for your light fixture and a rubber sealing ring to help you with the initial shaping.

Light lampshade

Cut 17 stakes each 60 cm (23⅝") long. To begin, use a bottle to help you shape the top. Fasten the stakes around the wide part of the bottle with a rubber sealing ring as in photograph 1. Leave about 5 cm (2") protruding beyond the rubber ring, then begin weaving in and out of the stakes as in photographs 2 and 3. After about 7 cm (2¾"), remove from the bottle (photograph 4). Bend the stakes outward and continue weaving, but more loosely (photograph 5). When the distance between the stakes is about 5 cm (2"), additional stakes must be incorporated. Place one extra next to each existing stake and, at one point, two extra (photograph 6). To estimate the length, measure what remains of the original stakes and add 4 cm (1½"). When the diameter of the lampshade reaches about 50 cm (19½"), bend the stakes inward and weave a very tight edge of about 10 cm (4") in

depth. When a weaving cane comes to an end, overlap the beginning of the new cane with the old one for about 1 cm (⅜") behind one of the stakes (photograph 7).

To make the looped edge, soak the stake ends in water for about 10 minutes. Allow about 10 cm (4") of stake for each loop and bend each stake into a loop by inserting it beside the stake after the next one.

Finally, trim any protruding canes down to 1 cm (⅜") (photograph 9). Paint the cane with wood stain.

Dark lampshade

Cut 13 stakes, each 40 cm (15¾") long. Use a bottle for the initial shaping, holding the stakes down with a rubber sealing ring (photograph 1). Leave 5 cm (2") protruding beyond the ring. Then begin weaving with the finer cane (photographs 2 and 3). After about 7 cm (2¾"), remove from the bottle (photograph 4), bend the stakes outward and begin shaping by weaving more loosely (photograph 5). After a further 7 cm (2¾"), bend the stakes inward slightly and weave more tightly. Then bend outward again and weave for about 8 cm (3") or until shade reaches a diameter of about 37 cm (14⅝"). To join on new lengths of cane, overlap the ends behind one of the stakes (photograph 7). Loops are made all around the outer edge to finish off the shade. Soak the stake ends for about 10 minutes first to soften them, then bend each stake into a loop and insert into the weave between it and the next stake. To fill the spaces, cut pieces 15 cm (6") long and add them into the looped edge. Trim ends.

To finish the top, weave in the ribs or, if you have an appropriate fixture, insert the ends into the rim. Paint with clear varnish.

It's a cinch

These belts are worked on the same principle as ordinary braiding. Just choose combinations of colors in jute or cotton and follow our instructions.

Seven-color belt
Materials Required:
Cotton macrame cord. Buckle. Leather scraps.

Making the belt
The finished belt (to wind twice around waist) is 2 cm ($\frac{3}{4}$") wide, 148 cm (58$\frac{1}{4}$") long [for 66 cm (26") waist]. However, the width may vary according to how tightly or loosely you braid. For a belt of this length, cut each strand about 3.70 m (4 yds) long. For a different length, (which you should try out by measuring with string first) work it out in the following way: establish the finished length and add $\frac{1}{4}$. If the finished length = 148 cm (58$\frac{1}{2}$"), $\frac{1}{4}$ = 37 cm (14$\frac{5}{8}$"). Therefore, 1 length = 185 cm (73$\frac{1}{8}$") and, as every strand is doubled, the entire strand measures 370 cm (146$\frac{1}{4}$"). Now double 6 of the strands and place them around the 7th as shown in the photograph. The braiding principle is the same as that shown on the far right. On this belt, every color runs in a zigzag down its length (this will help you to keep the strands

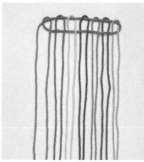

1 This photograph shows you how to begin work on the multi-colored belt. Double 6 strands and set them onto the 7th strand as shown. Draw them up firmly. Choose any color sequence you like.

2 The braiding technique is shown on the far right. For this belt, you have 7 strands or an odd number, which means that when braiding you always have 4 strands on one side and 3 on the other side.

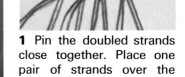

1 Pin the doubled strands close together. Place one pair of strands over the next pair along, moving from right to left.

2 Now braid the outer pair of red strands into the center and then the outer green pair, too. In the center, the pair of red strands now lies underneath the green pair.

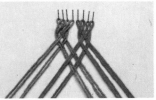

3 Then braid the next outer green pair of strands on the left into the center, then the right-hand outer red pair of strands.

4 Repeat this procedure with the next green and red pairs of strands.

5 Repeat once again; all the green strands are now on the right and all the red on the left.

6 Begin the braiding process again from the beginning.

in order). To finish, sew the ends together with a few stitches and secure with a strip of leather. Braid the belt loop with 6 single strands, each about 9 cm (3½″) long, sew a leather scrap over the ends. Then sew on the buckle.

Two-color belt
Materials Required:
Jute. Leather scraps. Narrow elastic. Toggle.

Making the belt
The finished belt is about 4.5 cm (1¾″) wide. The width may vary slightly according to how tightly you braid. Work out the length of thread as follows: establish the finished length and add ¼. For a 66 cm (26″) waist measurement, ¼ = 16.5 cm (6½″), therefore 1 length = 82.5 cm (32½″) and, as the strand is doubled, it is 165 cm (65″) long. Cut 4 red and 4 green strands and double them. Pin them close together (on an ironing board or carpet) as shown in photograph 1 and place the threads over one another as described. Continue to braid, following the photographs. When you have finished braiding, sew the ends of the strands together with a few stitches to secure. Cut 4 pieces of leather, each 5 cm x 5 cm (2″ x 2″) and 2 pieces of elastic each 5 cm (2″) long. Sew one piece of elastic to the center of one end of the belt as a loop. Draw other elastic through the toggle and then sew it to the other belt end. Sandwich the belt ends between the pieces of leather and stitch them on by hand with a decorative cross in the center.

99

From rags to riches

Braided rugs, unlike hooked or needle-made rugs, have no backing fabric or canvas. They are made entirely from remnants of fabric braided together and then sewn together in rounds. They are thick and durable, and very easy to make, even for the inexperienced. Wonderful color effects can be achieved by subtle mixing and matching.

Materials Required: Fabric. Carpet thread. Large tapestry needle or curved upholstery needle.

The most suitable fabrics are cottons, linens, and light woollens. It is best not to mix different types of fabric in one rug because of the difference in their wearing qualities.

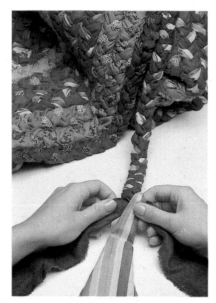

As you are braiding, fold the raw edges of the strips to the inside, so that they do not show on the right side and spoil the surface.

The pieces should be quite long, if possible, as they will be torn or cut into strips for braiding. You will need quite a lot of fabric. Our rug is 130 cm x 150 cm (51" x 59") and we used about 15 m (16 yds) of 90 cm (36") wide fabric.

Braiding the rug

Tear or cut all your fabric into long strips 6 cm–8 cm ($2\frac{1}{2}$"–3") wide. Now carefully plan the combination of colors in each braid as well as the colors of the whole rug.

To find the length of the starting braid for an oval rug, decide on the finished size of the rug and then subtract the width from the length. For our rug, this is 20 cm (8"), but we made a double row with a 40 cm (16") braid. To determine the length of the strips needed for each braid, estimate the finished length of the braid and multiply by $1\frac{1}{2}$. To make long strips, sew them together, right sides facing. Avoid lengthening two strips in the same place.

Anchor the ends firmly, fold the raw edges of the strips to the center as shown, then make a flat three-strand braid, being careful that the raw edges are on the inside. Braid only one round at a time so that you can decide when to change color to best effect in order to balance the colors.

Place finished braid, wrong side up, in an oval or a circle and sew to adjacent braid with doubled carpet thread. Fold the end to the wrong side and sew down. Begin next braid. End rug at desired size.

This rug was braided
in a combination
of plain and
patterned remnants. In each
braid, two of the three strips
are always plain and only one
patterned. This gives a spotted
effect over all the bands of color.

A braided sisal rug is ideal as a doormat – it's colorful and hard-wearing.

Here's a new craft to try!

Braided sisal in the round

Sisal braiding is easy — even children can do it — and here is a fascinating way of using sisal to make attractive rugs and mats. Lengths of sisal are first braided and then twisted and stitched into flat rounds. Finally, the rounds are stitched together to make decorative patterns.

Sisal is a practical material for making rugs. It is extremely hard-wearing, and easy to clean, as the finished structure of a braided rug is rather open and dirt falls right through. This makes them ideal for hallways, children's rooms, and places where the foot traffic is likely to be heavy.

Braided sisal can also be used to create beautiful table mats and covers. Hot plates won't harm the table and, after a meal, the mat is simply shaken to remove food fragments. Give free rein to your

Rounds can be stitched into a formal arrangement for a stunning hearth rug.

3-strand braiding

The technique is illustrated with pairs of strands in three colors so you can see where to place the strands. The rug rounds were braided in a single color, but tri-color rounds could certainly be used to produce a tweed. Note: It is important to keep the tension even.

Making the rounds

Six strands of 2-ply sisal were used to make the rounds for the rugs. Sisal is available in natural and a range of attractive colors. Cut the strands approximately $1\frac{1}{3}$ times the length of the required braid. A 30″ braid will make a round 9 cm ($3\frac{1}{2}$″) in diameter. A 60″ braid makes a 12.5 cm (5″) diameter round and a 90″ braid makes 15 cm (6″) diameter round.

creativity when planning the designs. Sisal can be obtained in bright colors but if you find that only the natural sisal is available, dye it to the color you require. Follow the manu-facturer's instructions.

Planning the design
Before starting to braid, draw a plan of the rug or mat on squared paper, indicating the colors to be used. Each circle must touch adjacent circles so that the sisal rounds can be stitched together.

Making a rug or mat
Make the rounds, laying them out according to your pattern. Stitch rounds together as shown at right.

Braiding and stitching sisal rounds

1 Knot three pairs of strands (2 red, 2 green, and 2 white) at one end and hang them from a hook. Place red pair to the right, green pair in the middle, and the white pair to the left.

2 Holding the red pair in your right hand and white pair in your left, bring the red pair to the middle over the green, being careful to keep the strands flat (do not let them twist).

3 Bring the white pair to the middle over the red. Continue to braid in this way by bringing outside strands from alternate sides to the middle. Knot or bind the braid at the end.

1 Cut lengths of sisal and knot them together at one end. Holding the strands by all the ends, dampen the strands in water to make them more pliable. Do not dampen ends.

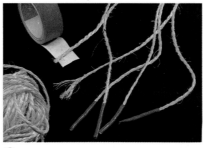

2 Bind the cut ends of the sisal with tape. This not only prevents fraying, but makes the strands easier to handle. The tape can be easily removed when the braiding has been completed.

3 Hang the knotted strands from a hook while braiding as this helps to achieve an even tension. If a hook is not available, the knot can be shut in a drawer to secure it.

4 At about 10 cm (4″) from the end, cut away one strand of each pair to reduce the bulk of the braid. Continue to braid with three single strands. Tie ends with a cut-off strand.

5 Starting from the tied-off end, bend the braid into a round and begin to stitch the braid to itself, using a heavy-duty thread. Use flat joining stitch and stitch on the wrong side of the work.

6 Work in a circle, making sure that the stitches are not pulled too tightly so that the round will not become distorted.
About 5 cm (2″) from the end of the braid, turn the knotted end toward the center of the round on the wrong side and cut it off straight across.
Stitch down the raw ends on the wrong side, making sure that no stitches show on the right side of the round.

A hard-wearing rug of braided sisal

Sisal is a strong, natural fiber which can be used to make bold rugs for country flooring.

Wound with string

The natural texture and the various colors of string give bangles a look which matches the mood of straw hats and summer clothes.

*

Materials Required: Plain plastic bangles in different thicknesses. All-purpose glue. Parcel string in a variety of colors.

Making the bangles

Cover the plastic bangles thickly with glue. Leave to dry slightly, then wind the string closely around the ring so that the plastic is completely covered.

Either finish the ring in one color or work in sections of different colors. For contrast, try mixing plain-colored string with two-colored string, or light colors with dark colors.

After finishing one color, cut off the string at the center of the back and glue down. Begin the new color just above it, making sure the end is not frayed. Leave to dry thoroughly.

Macrame is a very old technique of knotting yarn to produce a textured fabric. It is a craft which takes some time but is very rewarding. The originality of this macrame bag is in the material used – synthetic parcel string.

Tote bag in macrame
String along with fashion

Materials Required: Synthetic string, 2 140 m (155 yds) balls red, 1 ball beige.

Working the pieces

Straps (make 2): Cut 8 beige strands, each 8.5 m (9¼ yd) long. Fold each strand in half and knot together in pairs as shown in the diagram. Pin the knotted strands in a row as shown and work first one half, then the other in horizontal cording until each side measures 24 cm (9½"). Make bobbins by winding the ends of the strands around strips of cardboard.

Bag: Cut one strand 17.5 m (19½ yds) long and 25 strands 5 m (5½ yds) long from red string. Place one strap on the board so that the strands are hanging down. Secure a mounting cord over the strands as shown. Starting at the far left of the first strap end, mount the 17.5 m (19½ yds) strand so that 15 m (16¾ yds) hangs down at the left with the remaining 2.5 m (2¾ yds) next to it. Then double and mount four 5 m (5½ yds) strands between the first strand and the strap. Knot the strands of the first strap end over the mounting cord with half hitches, then double and mount 16 red strands, join the strands from the second strap with half hitches, and

finally double and mount the remaining 5 red strands. Make a bobbin at the end of each strand. The long strand is the knot bearer. Work horizontal bars of double half hitches throughout. Continue until the work measures 30 cm (11¾"). Repeat for second side.

Making the bag

Knot the strands at the bottom of each side together and weave in all ends. Join the sides from bottom to top with overcasting.

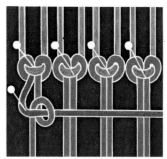

Knot pairs of strap strands together and pin them to the working surface. Pin the knot bearer in place.

Knot straps onto the mounting strand.

Cut off the bobbins and knot the two pieces together along the bottom edge.

Macrame– Mounting, Half hitches, Horizontal bars

You need a base of firm board or a sheet of polystyrene or styrofoam covered with fabric (a check pattern is helpful in keeping the rows straight), 2 table clamps to secure the board, pins, scissors, a tape measure or ruler, yarn or string, and a heavy-duty needle with a large eye.

Mounting strands

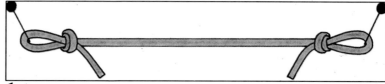

1 Cut a length of yarn about 45 cm (17¾") long. Make a knot at each end and stretch the yarn across the base. Fasten the strand securely with pins. This is the mounting cord.

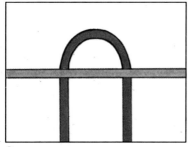

2 Fold another long piece of yarn in half and place the folded end under the mounting cord.

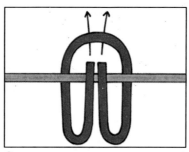

3 Take both ends of yarn up and over the mounting cord and through the loops.

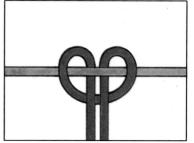

4 Now pull the ends of the yarn down and pull the knot tight. This is called mounting a strand.

Horizontal bar of half hitches

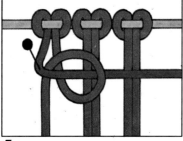

5 There are several different knots in macrame. The one shown here is called a double half hitch. Take the long strand (called the knot bearer) at left across the other strands to the right. Secure it at left with a pin. Hold the knot bearer with your right hand, keeping it taut. With your left hand, take the second strand and make a loop around the knot bearer as shown, pulling it tight to form a half hitch. Keep your tension even to make a regular pattern.

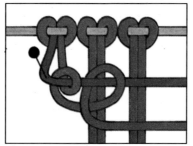

6 Make a second knot to form a double half hitch.

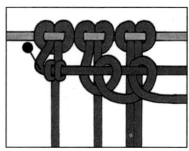

7 Make double half hitches with each strand.

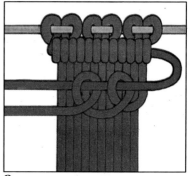

8 The second row is worked from right to left. Take the knot bearer across from right to left, securing it with a pin as before. Hold the knot bearer taut with your left hand and make knots around the knot bearer with your right hand. The following row is worked from left to right again. As you continue to work back and forth, a firmly corded fabric will be formed.

Square knot, Diagonal bar

Square knot

The square knot is made with two adjacent pairs of strands. The two outer threads are always placed alternately over and under the two center strands and each other.

Square knots can be worked singly, in horizontal rows, or in rows of alternating square knots. Alternating square knots are made by knotting together a pair of strands from each of two adjacent knots in the row above.

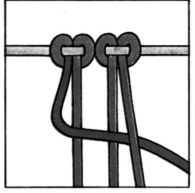

1 Place the left strand over the 2 center strands and under the right strand.

2 Place the right strand under the 2 center strands and over the left strand.

3 Place the left strand under the center strands, then the right strand over them as shown.

4 Make sure that the 2 center threads remain taut when the knot is pulled together.

Diagonal bar

A diagonal bar is made by knotting half hitches onto a strand slanting diagonally down to the left or right.

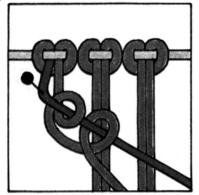

1 With each strand make a half hitch around the knot bearer. Pull knot tight.

2 Work from right to left in the same way. Always hold the knot bearer taut.

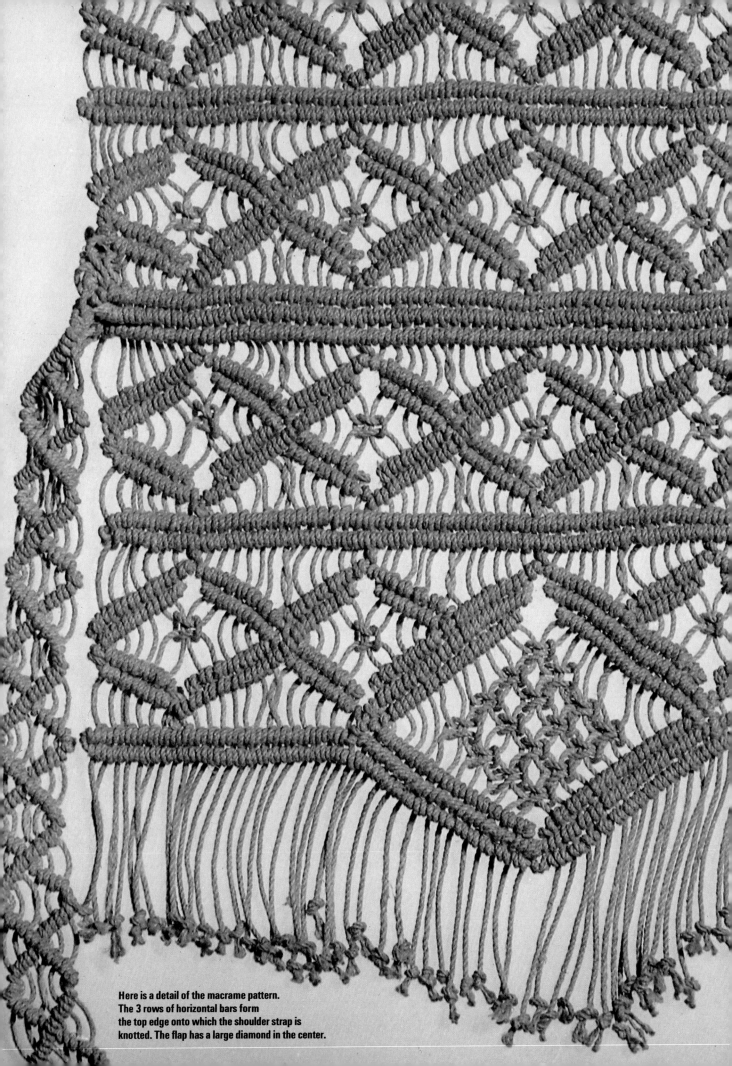

Here is a detail of the macrame pattern.
The 3 rows of horizontal bars form
the top edge onto which the shoulder strap is
knotted. The flap has a large diamond in the center.

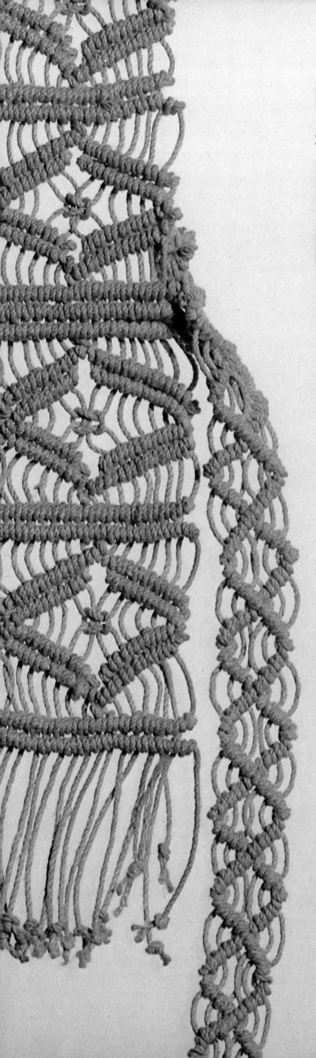

Shoulder bag in macrame

Lacy diamonds in twine

Although there are relatively few macrame knots, by combining them in a variety of ways, an abundance of patterns can be created. This shoulder bag is made in bars and square knots, using parcel string.

Size: 29 cm (11⅜") square.
Materials Required:
280 m (307 yds) parcel string. Mounting board.
Shoulder Strap: Cut 8 lengths of string 3 m (3¼ yds) in length. Work from the center out, knotting the diamond pattern in diagonal bars. When the strap measures 45 cm (17¾"), work the other half.
Bag: Cut 34 lengths of string 6.5 m (7⅛ yds) each and a mounting strand 14 m (15¼ yds). Make a simple knot at the center of the mounting strand and pin it to the base. Double the 34 strands of string and mount 17 strands onto the mounting strand to the right of the knot and 17 to the left. Work 1 horizontal bar, then work each of the 5 diamonds from the center out, working each diamond over 14 threads in diagonal bars. When the top half of the diamonds have been completed, make a square knot in the center of each one and then work the lower half. Work 2 horizontal bars over the mounting strand after each row of diamonds. After making 4 rows of diamonds, work 3 horizontal bars for the base, then 4 more rows of diamonds. For the top edge, work 3 horizontal bars. To begin the flap, work 1 row of diamonds and 2 rows of horizontal bars. In the next row, work the top half and square knots for the 4 outside diamonds, then in the center, work 3 diagonal bars to double the length to form a large diamond as shown. Fill the large diamond with square knots, then finish the small diamonds and work single diagonal bars for the large diamond. Finish with 2 horizontal bars. Trim strands and tie knots.
Finishing: Sew the sides together with string. Knot the strap to the top edge.

Attractive belts in macrame

Tie your outfit together

The diagram shows the belt patterns actual size. So that the position of the knots can be seen clearly, they are shown spaced wider apart than they will be when you knot the macrame cording.

YELLOW BELT
Materials Required:
Cotton cording. Mounting board.
Basic Knots: Diagonal bars and square knots.

Making the belt
Cut 13 strands, each measuring 3 m ($3\frac{1}{4}$ yds). Pin them to the board at their centers, so that you can work half the belt, then the other half. The left outer strand is the knot bearer. Work 1 row of diagonal bars, making a simple knot at the end of the row. In the second row, the next left outer strand is the knot bearer. Make a simple knot with this strand, then work a diagonal bar, making another simple knot at the end. Work the 3rd row with the next left outer strand in the same way.

Work a square knot with threads 3 to 6, counting from the left. Work 3 rows of diagonal bars from right to left. For each of these rows, the right outer strand is the knot bearer.

Repeat this pattern until you have 8 triangles. Knot the ends to secure them. Turn the work and knot the other half in the same way.

RED BELT
Materials Required:
Cotton cording. Mounting board.
Basic Knots: Diagonal bars and square knots.

Making the belt
Cut 12 strands, each measuring 3 m ($3\frac{1}{4}$ yds). Pin them to the board at their centers, so that you can work one half, then the other.

Use strand 6, counting from the left, as the knot bearer. Skip strand 7 and work a diagonal bar with the remaining 5 strands. Make a simple knot at the end. Use strand 7 as the knot bearer for the diagonal bar worked from right to left.

The second row begins at the center again. For the right diagonal bar, take the strand from the first knot of the previous left diagonal bar, skip 1 strand, and knot with the remaining 5 strands. For the left bar, the skipped strand becomes the knot bearer. Work a square knot with the center 4 strands, then work 4 rows of diagonal bars. For each row, use the outer left or right strand as the knot bearer and work 5 half hitches from both sides to the center. In the second row, cross the 2 center threads of the previous row. Work 2 more rows in the same way. The next 4 rows are worked from the center out.

Make a square knot, followed by 2 rows of diagonal bars. Repeat this pattern until $5\frac{1}{2}$ diamonds have been worked. Turn the work around and knot the other half in the same way. Knot the ends in groups of threads to secure them.

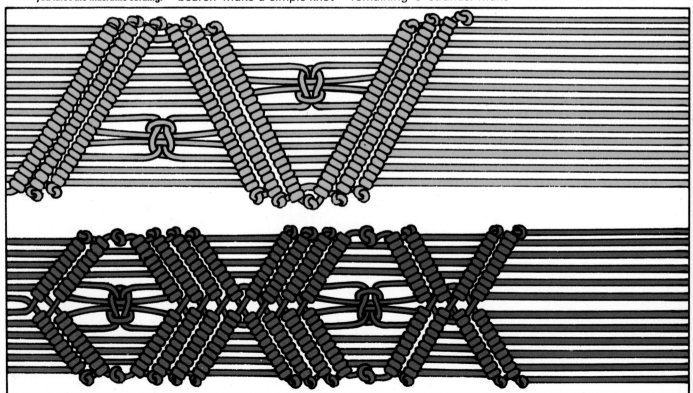

These two belts are worked in diagonal bars and square knots. Make them both to harmonize with a blouse or dress and wear them one above the other.

Macrame hammock
Swinging into summer

You can doze off comfortably and swing safely in this wide hammock made of strong synthetic string. It will take a fair amount of time and money to make, but will offer a lifetime of blissful relaxation.

Just below the rod, make 8 rows of 21 square knots in each of the different colored strings. The ends are bound together to suspend the hammock.

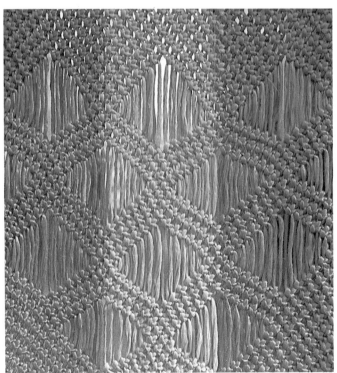

Here is a detail of the diamond pattern which forms the main part of the hammock. The diamond shapes are formed by 3 diagonal rows of square knots.

117

Materials Required:

Strong synthetic string in 500m or 550 yd balls: 2 balls green, 2 balls dark blue, 1 ball light blue. 2 solid curtain rods, each 1 m (1 yd) in length. 4 spherical rod ends. Dark blue enamel paint.

Mounting the threads

For each of the 5 stripes, measure out 32 strands of 14 m (15¼ yds) each. To facilitate the work, wrap each strand into a butterfly bobbin by winding the strand round your finger and thumb in a figure-eight and securing with an elastic band. The strand is released by a gentle pull.

Screw the rod ends onto the rods and paint both. Suspend one of the rods from 2 nails with thick string. Leave about 2.50 m (2¾ yds) of each strand hanging down for the suspension cords which will be worked at the end. Knot all the strands tightly onto the rod with half hitches (Diagram 1). Push all the threads close together.

Working the pattern

The main part of the hammock is worked in square knots (Diagram 2). The first 20 cm (8") consists of cords of square knots. With the first 4 strands, make 21 square knots, one below the other. Repeat with all the remaining strands (see top photograph on the previous page).

Now work 9 rows of alternated square knots: In the 1st row, make a square knot with each group of 4 strands. In the 2nd row, leave out the first 2 threads and make square knots with the following groups of 4. In the 3rd row, begin with the first 4 strands

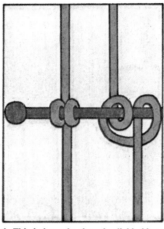

1. This is how the threads, divided into color groups, are knotted onto the rod with half hitches.

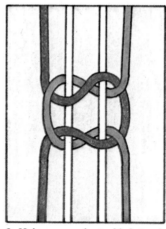

2. Make a square knot with 4 strands by tying the outer 2 around the inner 2 as shown. Pull tight.

3. Square knots can be alternated from row to row to form a staggered pattern as on the main part of the hammock.

again (Diagram 3).

In the 9th row, find the knot which is 5 knots down and 4 knots across. This is the apex of the first diamond in the pattern. Each side of a diamond has 8 knots. The shape is created by knotting

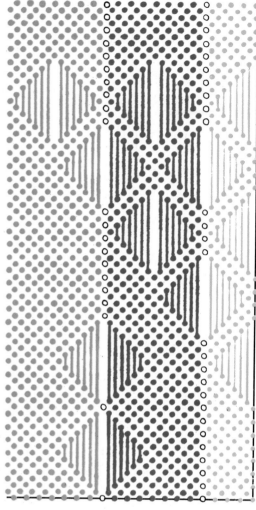

This diagram shows the first quarter of the main pattern. Repeat the pattern in reverse for the second quarter. Work the first half in reverse to make the second half.

● ● ●
Square knots
○ 2-colored knots
(change of color)

2 strands less from the center out in each of the following rows, leaving them hanging down. When 8 rows of knots have been worked, keep adding 2 more strands from the sides to the center in each row, pulling them taut. Work the other half of the diamond in reverse to match (see lower photograph on the previous page). Continue knotting, following the diagram at the top right, which shows a quarter of the pattern. Repeat the pattern in reverse for the 2nd quarter. When you reach the center, repeat the pattern again as a mirror image for the other half. On completion of the whole pattern, join on the rod at the other end with half hitches as before.

Working the ends

In the 1st row, gather all the strands of each color together. At about 8 cm (3"), wrap a strand around them about 10 times. In the 2nd row, divide the bundles of strands in half and combine each bundle with the color next to it, so that the wrappings are in a staggered line from the 1st row. In the 3rd row, all the light blue threads are grouped together, and at the sides, all the green and dark blue are grouped together. In the 4th row, divide the light blue threads and join them with the green and dark blue at the sides. In the last row, all threads are wrapped together.

Trim the strand ends to 45 cm (17¾"). Divide them into 2 bundles and overlap these by 15 cm (6") to form a ring. Bind the ring securely with a strand at least 1.5 m (1⅝ yds) long. Fasten off binding strand securely.

Add a pretty finish to a flowered shawl with macrame fringe

Fringe benefit

Materials Required:
Cotton fabric: 0.90 m (1 yd), 90 cm (36") wide. Cotton yarn: (shown actual-size below) 200 gm or 8 oz.

Macrame edging: Cut 4 mounting strands, each 2 m (2¼ yds) long. For the fringe, cut 316 strands each 80 cm (31½") long. Place the mounting strands in pairs, one below the other. Fold 300 of the fringe strands in half and knot onto the 2 upper mounting strands together. Work a horizontal bar of half hitches around the 2 lower strands together. Now work the top half of the diamonds from the center to the left edge. With first 10 strands, work diagonal bars down to the left, with next 10 strands, work 2 diagonal bars to the right, then repeat bars alternately to the left and right across (see photographs below). Make a square knot with the center

12 strands of each whole diamond, leaving the half diamond at the center of the edging. To complete the diamonds, begin at the center with 2 diagonal bars to the right and continue across as before.

Beginning at center, work other half in reverse.

For corner, make a right angle at center (see photograph). On each side, knot 5 new strands on last strand, 1 strand on each bar, and 1 strand on mounting strands. Connect the 2 sides with a semicircle of bars as shown.

Make an ordinary knot at the base of each diamond to hold the bars together. Sew in the ends of the mounting cords.

Shawl: Cut an 86 cm (34") fabric square and press 1 cm (⅜") to the inside all around. Fold into a triangle, baste, and stitch close to the edge. Attach the macrame edging with backstitch.

Here is a detail of the edging. It shows a diamond made with diagonal bars of half hitches and a square knot worked with twelve strands in the center.

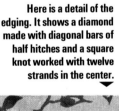

This photograph shows the way in which the corner is formed. Extra strands are mounted on and a semi-circle of bars connects the two sides.

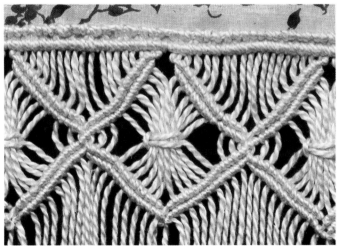

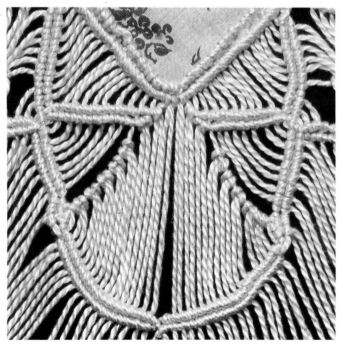

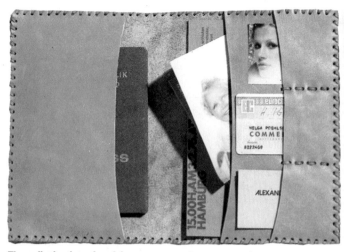

The gusset of the bag is given actual size. On the left side pattern diagram:

Gusset

Half-pattern line

The gusset of the bag is given actual size. Trace it onto tissue paper and glue this onto cardboard before cutting out.

The patterns for the bag and wallet are given here in diagram form. The numbers are centimeters, inch equivalents are on the right.

Note: Take the pattern with you when buying the leather to make sure you get the right size of skin. If you cannot obtain thongs, you can make them from thin strips of leather. The patterns are given in diagram form below.

Size: Bag: 21 cm x 62 cm ($8\frac{1}{4}$" x $24\frac{1}{2}$").
Wallet: 15 cm x 21 cm (6" x $8\frac{1}{4}$").

Materials Required: Both: Cow hide. Leather punch. Metal ruler. Leather cutting knife. Glue. Bag: Lining leather for flap. Leather thonging: 3 m ($3\frac{1}{4}$ yds), 4 mm ($\frac{3}{16}$") wide. 1 medium punch-in press stud. Wallet: Leather thonging: 2 m ($2\frac{1}{4}$ yds), 3 mm ($\frac{1}{8}$") wide.

Making the bag and wallet

Both: Enlarge the pattern pieces to actual size from the diagram. Cut out in cardboard. Check the skin for any blemishes and variation in color, then place the pattern pieces in a suitable position on the right side. Place weights onto the pattern and outline it in pencil. Making sure that you have a firm base on which to work, hold the ruler along the marked lines, press down firmly, and cut along the edge with the knife.

The wallet has lots of useful compartments for money, cards, etc.

Bag: For the curve on the pocket flap and the gusset, cut out carefully around the cardboard template. On the lining leather, mark the outline on the wrong side. On the lower, straight edge, add no seam allowance; to the other edges, add 2 cm ($\frac{3}{4}$"). Cut out. On the back of the bag, mark the line where the lining ends. Punch the upper part of the press stud into the lining leather, 2.5 cm (1") away from the point; press the lower part into the bag front, 16 cm ($6\frac{1}{4}$") from the edge.

Cover the wrong side of the flap and the lining with glue. Place the lower, straight edge of the lining onto the marked line on the bag and press firmly, smoothing upward. Cut off any lining that extends over the bag edge. Mark the positions of the thonging holes, 0.5 cm ($\frac{1}{4}$") from the edge and 1 cm ($\frac{3}{8}$") from center to center. Punch in the holes. Cut the thongs to a point at the ends to facilitate threading.

Begin by connecting the gusset to the sides, matching the letters. Leave the thong protruding a little and join with overcasting, pulling the thonging tightly. When one strip is finished, leave it hanging and start threading a new strip in the next hole. When the sides are finished, thong around the flap. Finally, trim the thong ends to measure the distance of one hole from another. Skive the ends on the underside with a sharp knife or razor blade to flatten them, cover one end with glue on the wrong side, and join together. In this way, the join will be unnoticeable. To flatten the edges of the bag, place them under a piece of wood and hammer them down.

Wallet: This is worked in basically the same way as the Bag, but the holes are placed 0.4 cm ($\frac{1}{8}$") from the edge and 0.8 cm ($\frac{5}{16}$") from center to center. Place the pieces together, matching the letters on the pattern, and join them with thonging as for the Bag.

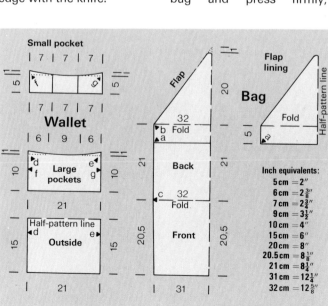

Small pocket
| 7 | 7 | 7 |
5

Wallet
| 7 | 7 | 7 |
| 6 | 9 | 6 |

Large pockets
10   d   e
      f   g
21

Half-pattern line
Outside   d   e
15
21

Flap   Fold   32   b a
Back   21
Fold   c   32
Front   20.5
31

Flap lining   Fold
Bag   20   5   b
Half-pattern line   21   20.5
Fold

Inch equivalents:
5 cm = 2"
6 cm = $2\frac{3}{8}$"
7 cm = $2\frac{3}{4}$"
9 cm = $3\frac{1}{2}$"
10 cm = 4"
15 cm = 6"
20 cm = 8"
20.5 cm = $8\frac{1}{8}$"
21 cm = $8\frac{1}{4}$"
31 cm = $12\frac{1}{4}$"
32 cm = $12\frac{5}{8}$"

Leather looks best

The clutch bag and wallet are made of cow hide thonged together through punched holes.

Materials Required: Beige leather: length to fit waist measurement plus 13 cm (5") for underlap by 5 cm (2") wide. Beige leather thonging: 260 cm (102½") long (for 70 cm (27½") waist) and 0.5 cm (¼") wide. Leather pieces in red and dark blue. Remnants of stranded embroidery cotton. Iron-on interfacing: 5 cm (2"), 90 cm (36") wide. Fine leather needle. 2 large press studs or snaps. Leather punch. Leather glue.

Working the appliqué

Trace the leather motifs onto tracing paper and glue them onto thin cardboard. Cut out the shapes, place them on the leather pieces, and draw around them. The end motif and the 2 scalloped shapes are cut out in red, the clover-shaped leaves in dark blue with 3 holes punched in them. Cut the belt to the required length, *i.e.* your waist measurement plus underlap. Trim the end of the belt to a curve to fit the shape of the end motif. Mark the position of the remaining motifs, distributing them at equal intervals along the belt and alternating the red with the blue. Glue on the motifs. Overcast around the edges. Mark the position of the embroidery motifs on the leather freehand or with tracing paper. Using 2 strands of cotton, the flowers are worked in buttonhole stitch, the stems in stem stitch, and the leaves in satin stitch. The flower centers, and small holes in the dark blue leaves are filled in with French knots.

Making the belt

Cut out the belt shape in iron-on interfacing and iron onto the back of the belt. Punch medium-sized holes all around the edge, 1 cm (⅜") apart and 0.5 cm (¼") from the edge. Draw the narrow beige thonging through these holes, keeping it taut. Begin at the top corner of the underlap, threading along the upper edge toward the front, around the curve and back again along the lower edge. It is important to keep the smooth side of the thonging uppermost. Fasten the thong ends at the back. Sew the press studs or snaps at each end of the underlap.

Waist line

Make this soft leather belt the focal point of an otherwise plain outfit. The motifs are appliquéd and embroidered with oddments of thread, using a fine leather needle. The edges are attractively finished with thonging.

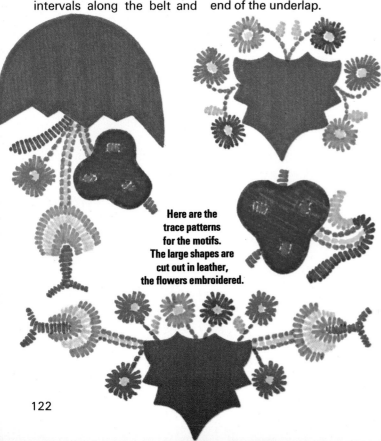

Here are the trace patterns for the motifs. The large shapes are cut out in leather, the flowers embroidered.

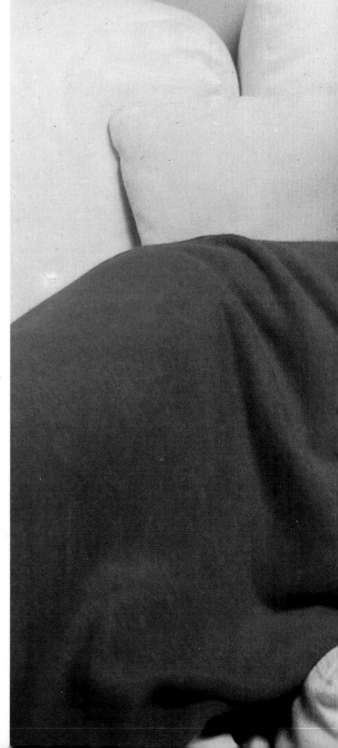

This soft belt with appliqué
motifs adds interest to
a plain dress. It fastens
at the front with two
press studs or snaps.

New life for leather leftovers

Here are five braided belts, each made in a different leather and color to show you how versatile they are. They are made from leather remnants in long strips. Shiny silver or white looks glamorous for evening wear, a soft, delicate suede enhances a plain day dress, while a smooth, sporty leather in a strong color is the perfect accessory for pants.

You will need very little leather for these braided belts. Remnants are ideal, provided that they are long enough, and we have used various types of leather to give a range of belts for all occasions. The belts are 3 cm (1¼″) wide (shown larger than actual size in the photograph).

Materials Required:
Buckle. Leather glue. Leather punch. Strip of leather or suede at least 12 cm (4¾″) wide. This width enables you to make

the ends of the belt from the remainder of the leather after cutting out the zigzag strips. For the required length, take your waist measurement and subtract 15 cm ($5\frac{3}{4}''$). This is the length of the braided part.

Choosing a buckle

Choose a buckle to match the belt in both style and color. Buckles are available in a range of sizes, colors, shapes, and prices at most needlework shops and large stores. Make sure that your buckle is not too heavy for the leather, otherwise it will pull down at the waist.

Hint: Before cutting into an expensive leather or suede, try making your first belt from a cheaper leather. When this one proves successful and you feel you have had a little practice, go on to a more ambitious belt — in silver leather for example. It is worth making several, as home-made belts are cheaper than ones you buy and you will have the added satisfaction of wearing a smart accessory you have made yourself.

◀ Silver leather, although rather expensive, is very elegant. The narrow silver buckle matches the belt beautifully.

Braiding and finishing a belt

Choose the leather for the belt carefully. Don't use a thick leather or you will be unable to cut it with scissors. On the other hand, it must be firm, otherwise it will stretch quickly with wear. Pull the leather slightly and you will be able to feel whether it stretches out of shape too easily.

Practice cutting, top-stitching, and punching holes on remnants of leather first for professional-looking results.

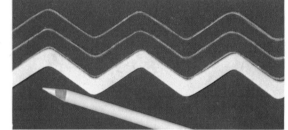

1 Trace the zigzag pattern (at left) onto heavy paper or cardboard and cut it out for the template. Draw around it on the wrong side of the leather with a pointed white pencil for dark colors or a lead pencil for light colors, extending it to the length required. 4 pencil lines = 3 strips.

2 Cut out the strips carefully with scissors. Place them one on top of the other as shown and tape the ends together. The strips will automatically fall into place when being braided.

3 For the end of the belt, cut two leather strips 2.8 x 15 cm (1⅛″ x 5¾″). Trim the ends of the braided strip and stick the layers together with glue. Place the two pieces together wrong sides together, catching in one end of the braided strip. Top-stitch all around the edge and punch a neat row of holes with a leather punch.

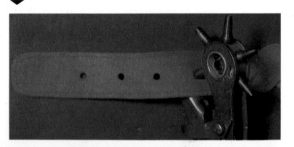

Trace this zigzag onto cardboard and you have your template.

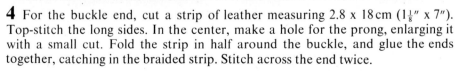

4 For the buckle end, cut a strip of leather measuring 2.8 x 18 cm (1⅛″ x 7″). Top-stitch the long sides. In the center, make a hole for the prong, enlarging it with a small cut. Fold the strip in half around the buckle, and glue the ends together, catching in the braided strip. Stitch across the end twice.

INDEX

Air-drying clay
  dolls 6
  modelling 7
Appliqué
  iron-on 9
  leather 122

Bag
  clutch, leather 120
  shoulder, macrame 112
  tote, macrame 108
Bar, macrame
  diagonal 111
  horizontal 110
Batik
  cushion 74
  dress 74
  how-to 76
  pillow 74
  scarf 74
  wall hanging 75
Bead
  belt 34, 36, 37
  bracelet 42
  button 43
  choker 42
  curtain 45
  necklace 38, 42
  weaving
    diagonal lines 44
    flat beading 35, 44
    loops 36
    spiral pattern 35, 44
    tubular chain 35, 44
Belt
  appliquéd leather 122
  bead 34, 36, 37
  braided 98, 124
  clear-cast embedded 12
  fastening, making a 14
  leather 122, 124
  macrame 114
  woven 83, 90
Block printing 48
Book, covering a 20
Bouquet
  pine cone flower 32
  plastic flower 15
Box
  découpage 28

painted wooden 64, 66
  shell-covered 31
Bracelet
  bead 42
  painted wooden 61
  wrapped 107
Braided
  belt 98, 124
  rug 100, 102
Braiding
  eight-strand 99
  leather 126
  seven-strand 98
  three-strand 104
Button, bead 43

Cane weaving 96
Card weaving 84
Cardboard party train 25
China, painted 58
Choker, bead 42
Clay, air-drying
  dolls 6
  modelling 7
Clear-cast embedding
  belts 12
  how-to 14
Clutch bag, leather 120
Curtain, bead 45
Cushion
  batik 74
  block-printed 48

Découpage
  box 28
  how-to 30
  tray 28
Doll, air-drying clay 6
Dress, batik 74
Dyeing yarn 80

Eight-strand braiding 99

Fabric
  book cover 20
  painting 71
Fish lure necklace 38
Flower
  painted plastic 15
  pine cone 32
Frame, picture

painted 62
  shell 31
Fringe, macrame 119

Glass painting 54
Glassware, painted 54

Half hitch 110, 111
Hammock
  macrame 116
  woven 92

Iron-on appliqué 9

Lampshade
  cane-woven 96
  paper 18
Leather
  belt 122, 124
  clutch bag 120
  wallet 120
Linoleum block printing 48

Macrame
  bars
    diagonal 111
    horizontal 110
  belt 114
  fringe 119
  hammock 116
  knots
    half hitch 110, 111
    square 111, 118
  shoulder bag 112
  tote bag 108
Mitering a corner 94

Napkin, potato printed 50
Nature crafts
  dyeing yarn 80
  pine cone flowers 32
  shell mosaics 31
Necklace
  bead 38
  fish lure 38
  sequin 40

Painting
  china 58
  fabric 71
  glass 54
  wood 61, 62, 64, 66

INDEX

Paper
    book cover 20
    découpage 28
    lampshade 18
    party train 25
Party train, cardboard 25
Picnic case, lining a 22
Picture frame
    painted 62
    shell-covered 31
Place mat, woven 94
Plastic
    belt buckle 12
    flowers, painted 15
Potato printing
    how-to 52
    napkin 52
    place card 52
    tablecloth 50
Printing
    block 48
    linoleum block 48
    potato 50

Rag rug
    braided 100
    woven 86
Rug
    braided 100, 102
    woven rag 86

Scarf, batik 74
Sequin necklace 40
Seven-strand braiding 98
Shawl, painted 69
Shell mosaic 31
Shoulder bag, macrame 112
Skirt, painted 69
Square knot 92, 111, 118

Tablecloth
    block-printed 48
    potato-printed 50
Tablet weaving 84
Techniques, illustrated
    air-drying clay, modelling 7
    batik 76
    bead weaving 35, 36, 44
    block printing 48
    book covering 21
    braiding 98, 99, 104, 126

    cane weaving 96
    card weaving 84
    china painting 60
    clear-cast embedding 14
    découpage 30
    dyeing yarn 80
    fabric painting 71
    macrame 110, 111, 118
    mitering a corner 94
    paper lampshade making 19
    picnic case lining 23
    pine cone flower making 33
    plastic flower painting 17
    potato printing 52
    raised-design painting 65
    tablet weaving 84
    weaving 88, 89
Three-strand braiding 100, 104
Tote bag, macrame 108
Tray, découpage 28

Vinyl-coated
    book cover 20
    picnic case lining 22

Wall hanging, batik 75
Wallet, leather 120
Weaving
    basic techniques 89
    cane 96
    card 84
    rag rug 88
    tablet 84
Wood, painted
    box 64, 66
    bracelet 61
    picture frame 62
Woven
    belt 83, 90
    hammock 92
    place mat 94
    rug, rag 86

Yarn dyeing 80